THE MOON THAT HIDES A SECRET

Simon Lewis

Order this book online at www.trafford.com
or email orders@trafford.com

Most Trafford titles are also available at major online book retailers.

Print information available on the last page.

ISBN: 978-1-4907-5634-9 (sc)
ISBN: 978-1-4907-5636-3 (hc)
ISBN: 978-1-4907-5635-6 (e)

Library of Congress Control Number: 2015905439

Trafford rev. 07/01/2015

 www.trafford.com

North America & international
toll-free: 1 888 232 4444 (USA & Canada)
fax: 812 355 4082

CONTENTS

FOREWORD

I can describe my journey as exciting and very much filled with questions. These questions were to lead me to research the paths of the unknown. I have always been fascinated by the Moon and everything that it entailed. The space missions were just amazing, the technology incredible. In the early 1990's I joined a UFO group. It was to become a journey that would lead me to conclusions I could never of imagined thinking of before.

UFO (Unidentified Flying Object) research is about investigating a sighting and following through with detailed accounting of information. You don't just jump to a conclusion; you have to work hard at proving it.

I joined specialist organisations connected with aircraft to further my knowledge. This became useful for identification of objects in the sky, as well as gaining respect. One of my first published articles was about aircraft identification. This was to help the public have an understanding of what was flying above their heads. It was not long before I started meeting different people from industries related with flight and space exploration. This soon boosted my interest in the Apollo Moon landings, as well other Moon related subjects. I started to buy book after book about the Moon, as well as historic photos and documents. The internet soon became a great place to buy space memorabilia from auction sites. It did not take long to publish a few articles on Moon anomalies; this soon became my biggest interest.

As time passed it was clear something was being hidden from the public domain. It soon became a vast area of discrepancies, which would mean more work. Joined by others we started to unfold the truth, which would change everything about the Moon and our views.

To keep up to date with my latest research, please take a look at my Facebook page:
www.Facebook.com/TheTwoFacedMoon

INTRODUCTION

The subject of life on other planets has always fascinated me. We have the capability to explore outside our own atmosphere and go further than ever before. As with the first space rockets that orbited the earth, the men that walked on the moon and the probes that visited distant planets, our presence beyond earth was becoming known.

Throughout history there seems to be a clear indication that maybe we were already a galactic member of other worlds. Archaeology has brought us incredible insights into the past from early man, to giant pyramids, to treasures untold. All this has given us a chance to discover who and what we are. If I was to look at the most astounding thing that has changed our thinking it would be religion - the belief in a God which has shaped all our lives from day one.

We have battled with each other and still do, we are only just growing. We face a future of uncertainty and flow with the positive and negative that is our world.

The question is... are we the only beings that live in the vast universe that surrounds our little planet? If I was to be outspoken, I would say NO! Over the last 24 years I have researched UFOs, moon anomalies, and anything that attracts attention. For all the people I have met from the ordinary to the pilots, astronauts, scientists and doctors, they all kept saying "We are not alone". The evidence outweighs anything I have ever come across before. This brings me to a subject that I have followed for a long time and has brought me many surprises, one word "Apollo" - the achievement to land on the Moon and return. As Neil Armstrong said....

"That's one small step for a man, one giant leap for mankind"

These words would echo forever in our minds. The Moon landings would for the first time give us a chance to look at another world first hand.

The general discoveries were amazing, so many types of rock, telling us of the violent past that created worlds. In fact the Moon revealed that it was a treasure trove of information on our journey of knowing. Of course there had to be the critics who would talk about the cost, hoaxes and stages etc. Generally people would not ask questions if it was not for the opinions uttered by the few:

1962   Doctor Carl Sagan - Adviser on ET life to the US forces) was convinced the moon was occupied.

1968   Major Patrick Powers (Head of the United States Army Development programme) said "Be prepared to fight for the privilege to land."

1968   Patrick Moore and Barbara Middlehurst (Chronological Reported Lunar Events) published hundreds of documented reports of unusual activity on the Moon spanning centuries.

1975   Maurice Chatelain (Space scientist, a designer of the Apollo spacecraft, NASA Chief of Communications for the Apollo space craft) said that Armstrong and Aldrin talked of UFOs hovering over head.

1970   Doctor Farouk El Baz (Former NASA scientist) said not every discovery was made public and astronauts would talk in code. For example Santa Claus meant UFO.

2008   Edgar Mitchell (Apollo 14 astronaut) revealed that we have made contact with aliens.

This list of people who 'say it as it is' just continues. Are we to believe they are all mad or are we finally waking up to the truth? Let's look at what evidence could possibly exist. All the Moon landings were filmed and photographed, including recordings of conversations.

Firstly I would like to discount the hoax theory. Ham radio for instance picked up the signals from the Moon. We now have pictures of the landing areas. In fact what a fantastic relief for NASA that everybody focussed on a hoax and nobody questioned what they were there for.

I think John F Kennedy knew exactly why we were landing on the Moon and it was not to look at rocks. Apart from the show down between the USSR over who got there first, the rest was who got what first. History was made and in 1972, Apollo 17 lands for the last time.

It doesn't just end like that...

When you look at the discrepancies they are huge. We all love the internet these days and it is basically an information highway. But look carefully as what seems normal at first, may not be what it appears. How many of us have noted that there are different dubbed versions of Apollo footage? There are so many I have lost count. Was this poor editing or a game? Conversations between Apollo astronauts have revealed unusual words...

"Are those your footprints?"

"Look like tracks?"

"Unusual fluorescence?"

My goodness those were brave words. Many of the photographic images taken were outstanding and also revealed a lot.

At the time, they used the best camera technology available. Hasselblad cameras gave superb detail. I find it almost crazy to think for one minute that the US would spend trillions of dollars just to look at rocks.

We have China and India very much reaching out to the Moon. You don't go all the way back unless there is something worth going for. Every film and every picture tells a story and it would seem a percentage of people made it clear from the start that we are not alone.

So let's say the Moon is inhabited, let's say we have made contact and agreements have been made. Apart from total religious melt down, what is it all about?

This is my theory. Going to the Moon was also to prove a point to someone else, and not the USSR. Perhaps Star Trek has some truths. Prove you can land on the Moon and join the galactic club. An even more wild idea would be that everything is a game. Here we are on planet earth. There are a few that know for certain that alien life exists and that it is very much advanced. You could look at Roswell as an alien mistake - hostages and technology. We could also look at the fact that all the time we have been manipulated from somewhere else, by another or many different ET's.

From the beginning of history all the signs indicate that we have made contact. Are we all really that daft? Open your eyes and look at everything again!

In conclusion, the Apollo missions were a show of our ability to achieve the impossible. I am certain with help from somewhere else. The technology was amazing considering this was 1969. All the astronauts were of military backgrounds and trained to be superhuman. All the time they were also told to be silent. They were still human, but held in a system of control. Did you know that quarantine after a mission also meant checking that an astronaut hadn't lost his marbles? Not good having an astronaut coming back telling all. This book will give you an insight into the other side of the story, with old and new evidence leading us to an earth shattering truth.

We are not alone!

Simon Lewis

Author of 'The Two Faced Moon' and revised edition.

Also featured in 'Two Faced Moon' DVD.

Former writer for UK magazines and collector of Apollo and space related memorabilia.

CHAPTER 1

THE JOURNEY BEGINS

On the 20th July 1969 the whole world watched live on television as Neil Armstrong set foot on the Moon. Armstrong was ex aviator veteran of the Korean War and former pilot of the Gemini 8 missions. His skills and experience finally gave him the position of the Commander of Apollo 11 where he was joined by crewmates Micheal Collins and Buzz Aldrin. Armstrong and Aldrin landed on the Moon in the Lunar Module [Eagle] whilst Collins orbited the Moon in the Module [Columbia]. Armstrong will always be remembered for those famous words *"That's one small step for a man, one giant leap for mankind."* The rest is history - or the history they wanted you to hear.

Long before any Moon landings of any kind, observations of unusual activity had been recorded on the Moon and from this came the term "Chronological reported lunar events." The Moon it seemed was not the dead body we were all made to believe. The official report which was documented by Patrick Moore and Barbara Middlehurst in 1968 and updated in 1971 documented a different story. It was an amazing insight into Moon activities over the centuries.

As early as 1671 on the 12th November, D Casino observed small whitish clouds around the crater P Tatus and in more recent years, the NASA Lunar orbiter [Plate 48 NASA Lunar Orbitor V NO MR

168] photographed what seemed to be cone shaped clouds as well as Cirrocumulus clouds in an area of the crater Vitello, Mare Imbrium. The crater has a diameter of 30 miles and walls rising 4,500 feet and is surrounded by small hills and craters. It would seem almost ridiculous to suggest we were observing a warm frontal system but the clouds do seem to show rippling effect as they pass over the crater. NASA refers to the picture as 'having marks on it'. What the picture does create is argument and debate because those marks could possibly be clouds. This picture is one of many unusual pictures showing strange events on and around the Moon and this makes it harder to explain them as just being errors or marks and in some cases transmission problems. The crater Alphonsus has had well documented evidence of unusual blur when monitored. N.A Kozyrev, of the Crimean Astrophysical Observatory in the U.S.S.R. was monitoring the crater Alphonsus using a 50inch reflector on the 3rd November 1958 when he noticed that the central peak had become blurred. What had been quite notable was the reddish cloud on the central peak which soon went very bright and then dim. Alphonsus soon returned to its normal self. It seems observations by astronomers in past centuries were well documented and good records kept. One of the main talking points was red spots, red streaks and bright areas etc.

These have been observed around craters such as Plato and Aristachus. Observations go back hundreds of years and these activities lead us to ask questions.

Clouds moving over Crater Vitello.
[NASA Lunar orbiter V NO, MR168]

Earth clouds

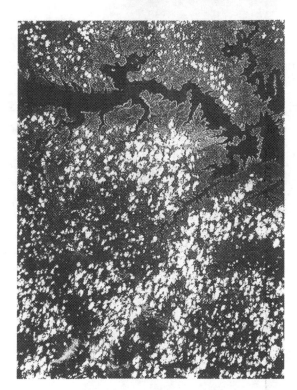

There have been more than 300 reports relating to the Aristachus area alone. Aristachus stands on a rocky plateau, with walls 2000ft high. As early as March 1783, W.Hershel and Lind observed red spots within the vicinity of the crater. Observations continued with Shroter and Van Bruhl from 1784 to 1787 noting unusual bright areas of light in and around craters. Then on 13th February 1835, again unusual bright spots were observed by Gruithuisen.

It is almost tempting to say that going to the Moon in 1969 was more than just a Cold War statement; perhaps it was to make observations of the Moon's many secrets that others had reported. Sightings continued throughout the decades, all being documented and recorded.

In 1963 on the 30th October two observers, Greenacre and Bom, saw three-red spots, one inside Aristachus and the other two nearby in the Schroter Valley. The entire display lasted over 45 minutes.

The Apollo 11 Mission even reported a strange fluorescence towards Aristachus, as the following conversation revealed:

Armstrong: "Hey, Houston, I'm looking north up towards Aristachus now and I can't really tell at that distance whether I am looking at Aristachus, but there's an area there that is considerably more illuminated than the surrounding area. It just has, seems to have a slight amount of fluorescence to it."

Houston [McCondles]:	"Roger, eleven, we copy."
Aldrin:	"Looking out the same area now, well at least there is one wall of the crater that seems to be more illuminated than the others. I'm not sure that I am really identifying any phosphorescence, but that definitely is lighter than anything else in the neighborhood."
Houston [McCondles]:	"Can you discern any difference in the color of the illumination and is that an inner or outer wall from the crater? Over."
Aldrin:	"I judge an inner wall in the crater."
Collins:	"No there doesn't appear to be any colour involved in it Bruce."

A crater of
mystery - Aristarchus

Twenty minutes passed and the signal from Apollo 11 was lost as it moved around the dark side. When it reappeared, nothing else was said. You would have thought that this particular event would have made great news considering how many observations had been recorded in and around Aristachus, but alas no. You immediately wonder 'why go to the Moon, see amazing things and then keep it a secret?' My goodness the Moon is not exactly just down the road, yet the conversation seems to be lost to the general public for whatever reason.

We have observed unusual activity from Prolemoreus, Mare Crisium, Posidonius, Plato-to-Bessel, Tycho, Longrenus and the list goes on. I find it frustrating that this has been taking place over a long period of time and we are still in a situation where the public are not informed of these facts. Surely we should be made more aware of these anomalies and what I consider to be very important pieces of information. I found it difficult to obtain data as it was not as readily available as it should be.

NASA including the Russians, photographed and most probably filmed unusual phenomena on the Moon, which has never been made public knowledge. It seems to still stay a secret rather than to be made a historic scientific find. You feel as though somebody did not want information releasing and that it was best for them to stay silent than create a storm.

As you can see from the next conversation, the questions outweigh the answers. The mission was that of Apollo 16 on 22nd April 1972.

Duke: "Tony, what is the other peak?"

Capsule   "Right of the cosmic ray experiment."
Communicator:

Duke: "Ok, I'll cross F-11 250 at 15"

Young: "Ok, Houston, I just picked up this white rock, but it has a black layer on the back of it, a thick black glass and it's about [garble] specimen."

Capsule   Scramble. "Hey, fellow, Ken was just flying
Communicator: over and he saw a flash on the side of Descortes-he probably got a glint of you?"

Duke: "Oh sure, that's us. Men of miracles. We're dusty."

Young: "Don't step right here, Charlie, there's a splatter, a glass splatter. A whole big bubble of it, isn't it?"

This particular conversation makes it quite clear that the flash seen wasn't anything to do with the astronauts on the Moon. I am quite sure they were well trained in observation as well as conclusions.

Back in 1972, NASA announced that it would be studying LTP [Lunar Transient Phenomena]. Basically NASA would require anyone who had the equipment and knowledge to carry out a study of the Moon in detail. There were thirty two responses; these people would have to study four areas of the Moon that had shown LTP. The frustrating factor of this initiative was that not enough people reported back therefore it came to a rather abrupt end. This just left us with the 1968 report and 1971 updates as documented evidence.

The Apollo Missions did find all kinds of interesting things which were made public. This included rocks, dust and crystals etc. as part of the many 75,000 lunar samples that were collected. Studies carried out on the majority of the pieces found materials that were composed of glass drops from a meteorite, to a large breccia encased in molten rock. Many of the materials would be ideal for industry, including silicon for computers and soil which could be used to produce glass in a low gravity environment.

An interesting factor is the abundance of materials. Derived from Moon dust, NASA scientists recently discovered that Helium 3 holds the key to a cheaper energy source. Dr John Santarius of Wisconsin University came to the conclusion that 25 tons of Helium 3 could power the whole of the United States for a year. When you consider the Space shuttle payload bay can carry that amount, things become more plausible.

It is rather amazing how the Moon is more shrouded in secrecy now than it was before we landed on it. Perhaps our closest neighbour has more to offer than we would like to make public? The information that is released is always trivial news - never a big headline. In some cases it does make the bigger pages of the newspapers, such as the story of water being found on the Moon.

What is interesting is how a number of astronomers and scientists have in the past clearly said we would never find water on the Moon. On the 3rd December 1996, frozen water had been found deep in a crater on the south pole. The probe [Clementine] which was military, discovered an area of water twice the size of Puerto Rico and had a depth of 1.3 kilometers. This finding of water changes everything if you want to colonise the Moon. This whole thing about water reminds me of what was actually discovered back in the 1970's on the Apollo Missions which caused great debate at the time.

NASA Assistant Director of Lunar Science Richard Allenby quoted *"There is no evidence in the rocks or geochemistry that water exists"*. This statement was soon to be quashed when Dr. John Freeman and Dr. H. Ken Hills announced that great eruptions of water vapour clouds had been detected which covered an area of 100 square miles of the Moon's surface and had lasted 14 hours. When you consider the strange photographs of clouds seen on the Moon you can easily make the connections. NASA decided to explain the whole event off as being water tanks from the Apollo descent stages. The science team reacted by pointing out that both the Apollo 12 and 14 missions had been located over 180km away so they could not have brought the water themselves. Things really started getting heated when NASA announced it was merely 'pee' released from the space capsules. The Apollo 17 Mission on December 29th 1972 reveals once again an interesting conversation mentioning water:

Capsule Communicator: "Roger. America, we're tracking you on the map here, watching it."

Lunar Module Pilot: "O.K., Al Buruni has got variations on its floor. Variations in the lights and in its albedo. It almost looks like a pattern as if the water were flowing up on a beach. Not in great areas, but in small areas around the southern side, and the part that looks like the water-washing pattern is a much lighter albedo, although I cannot see any real source for it. The texture, however, looks the same."

Capsule Communicator: "America, Houston. We'd like you to hold off switching to OMNI Charlie until we can cue you on that."

Commander: "Wilco."

Lunar Module Pilot: "O.K 96:03. Now we're getting some clear –looks like pretty clear high watermarks on this   "

Commander Module Pilot: "There's high watermarks all over the place there."

Lunar Module Pilot: "On the north part of Tranquillitatis. That's Maraldi there, isn't it? Are you sure we're 13 miles up?"

Capsule Communicator: "You're 14 to be exact, Ron."

Lunar Module Pilot: "I tell you there's some mare, ride or scarps that are very, very sinuous- just passing one. They not only cross the low planar areas but go right up the side of a crater in one place and a hill in another. It looks very much like a constructional as I would want to see it."

Above: The South Polar Region of the Moon.
Below: Clementine probe which photographed ice.

Things do not make sense, so many astronomers and scientists seem to want to stand out from the crowd and yet something holds them back. The Moon is so close and yet so far from our minds, it holds more secrets and has the answers we probably are looking for. The whole water debate was just brushed aside and yet decades later we find water officially accepted and found by Clementine.

Without a doubt technology has brought the Moon closer than ever with the advance of computers and general telescopes. The telescopes available to the general public are superb and can see most night sky objects with a trained eye and patience. Computers and digital technology combined give us pictures and film. With new technology advancing all the time, the telescope now sees further and clearer than before. More people are reporting unusual phenomena. I think it's time to go back to the Apollo Missions and look at everything again in more detail.

The possibilities are endless, especially with new players such as China and India releasing new footage and images of the Moon. Even Russia envisages returning to the Moon and building a lunar base. At last it seems like the truth is about to be revealed.

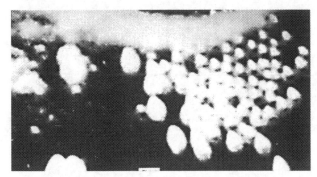

Crater Ritter [Area blow up] showing cloud.
Lunar orbiter photo MR81

CHAPTER 2

THE SECRET

So why did we go to the Moon? Was it a Cold War thing or maybe something else? Let's imagine that going to the Moon was more about who got the treasure first. We have already looked at the facts on Chronological reported lunar events, which on their own were one good reason to go to the Moon.

But what if an alien species was already on the Moon?

On 14th December 1968, Major Patrick Powers [Head of the United States Army Space Development Program], made some bold statements: *"Human landings may be challenged"* and *"The first man to reach the Moon must be prepared to fight for the privilege of landing."*

Back in 1962, Dr Carl Sagan was the adviser on extraterrestrial life to the US forces. He stated that mankind must face the probability that beings from elsewhere in the Universe have, or have had, bases on the averted side of the Moon.

Those were very powerful words for such high profile people at the time. They were aware of something that was not public knowledge then and even now.

I think the most interesting discussed phenomena of the 1950's was the artificial bridge. It was the late John O'Neil, former Science Editor of the New York Herald Tribune who really caused a big stir in lunar observations. In July 1953, he reported what he called a 'gigantic artificial arch' 12 miles long known as the 'Lunar Bridge'. This was later confirmed by Dr H.P. Wilkins at the Mount Wilson Observatory, USA. The bridge was viewed a month later under good conditions but had disappeared.

It is interesting that so many people were hungry to discover the Moons secrets and until we landed there, they were not willing to divulge anything. The thoughts that must have been going through their minds must have been amazing.

Another interesting yet controversial story relates to the spikes on the Moon. On November 18th 1966, a lunar orbiter left Cape Kennedy. Three days later, from a height of 30 miles, the instruments telephoto lens was focused on the Moon's surface and the camera activated. On a small area of the Sea of Tranquility, a plain just off the Moons centre, the camera picked up six spike-like projections, casting shadows across the dusty surface. They were called 'some of the most unusual features of the Moon ever photographed' by the scientists in charge of the project. However, they felt the spikes to be natural. Mr William Blair, a Seattle anthropologist and a member of the Boeing company's biotechnology unit, thought otherwise. He maintained they were in a geometric pattern *"similar to columns built by man"*.

Without a doubt, the Apollo Missions were an incredible achievement. To go all the way to the Moon and back again and return alive said something about us as human beings. Great courage and dedication paid off, but were we all really being given the truth? So many miles, so many new frontiers, but for who's benefit? There is one big problem with the Apollo program. Apart from the cost, it was generally a show of what America was capable of and if that meant keeping secrets at the same time, then why not? What we found was probably difficult to deal with and with most of the world watching, NASA had two channels, one for the public and the other for them, so in other words: 'See anything unusual that may cause a stir then communicate on a different frequency and keep it a secret'.

This form of censoring a transmission between astronaut and M.C. is called the 'delayed-tape technique' which allows a delay of a number of minutes before the public can hear the transmissions. The only problem NASA had was amateur radio operators who were able to pick up these censored communications. One example of covering up conversations comes from the Apollo 11 Mission where Neil Armstrong and Buzz Aldrin saw something very spectacular. The story is incredible because their conversation talks of them being observed from nearby hills when they were on the Moon. Otto Binder a former NASA space program member claimed that conversations had taken place on the Apollo Missions of reports of unusual activities outside the spacecraft; these were of course deleted by NASA so no further questions could be asked.

Even more unusual is that Dr Farouuk El Baz's [NASA foremost scientist] statement back in the 70's was that not every discovery had been announced and that NASA most likely used codes in some of their mission-control conversations with the astronauts.

The following Apollo 16 conversation highlights this point:

Capsule Communicator: "What about the albedo change in the subsurface soil? Of course you saw it first at Flagg and were probably more excited about it there. Was there any difference in it there—and Buster and Alsep and LM?"

Duke: "No. Around the Alsep it was just in spots. At Plum it seemed to be everywhere. My predominant impression was that the albedo was [garble] than the fine cover on top."

Capsule Communicator: "O.K. just a question now for you, John. When you got to halfway, or even thought it was halfway, we understand you looped around south, is that right?"

Young: "That's affirm. We came upon-Barbera."

I am sure you would agree that this conversation was difficult to follow, but intended for certain ears only. It clearly showed the use of code when passing on sensitive information. In the following conversation communications between Apollo 17 and mission control soon change to code:

Lunar Module Pilot: "What are you learning?"

Capsule Communicator: "Hot spots on the Moon, Jack?"

Lunar Module Pilot:	"Where are your big anomalies? Can you summarize them quickly?"
Capsule Communicator:	"Jack, we'll get that for you on the next pass."
Command Module Pilot:	"Hey, I can see a bright spot down there on the landing site where they might have blown off some of that halo stuff."
Capsule Communicator:	"Roger. Interesting. Very- go too KILO. KILO."
Command Module Pilot:	"Hey, its gray now and the number one extend."
Capsule Communicator:	"Roger. We got it. And we copy that it's all on the way out down there. Go to KILO on that."
Command Module Pilot:	"Mode is going to HM. Recorder is off. Lose a little communication there, huh? Okay, there's bravo. Bravo, select OMNI. Hey, you know you'll never believe it. I'm right over the edge of Orientale. I just looked down and saw the light flash again."
Capsule Communicator:	"Roger. Understand."
Command Module Pilot:	"Right at the end of the rille."
Capsule Communicator:	"Any chance of- ?"
Command Module Pilot:	"That's on the east of Orientale."
Capsule Communicator:	"You don't suppose it could be Vostok?" [This was a Russian probe]

You do feel a sense of panic as NASA suddenly realised that they might not be the only ones on the Moon. Or were they expecting this from the start? Taking things one step at a time and ensuring the public were not aware of anything. So we have looked at the use of code, which is very useful if you want to hide something.

On the Apollo 16 Mission, conversations and even film show us that things are not what they seem. NASA has without a doubt gone to great lengths to show us all a well edited version of the Moon landings. The sad factor is that this great achievement was to benefit only a few. You do wonder why so many secrets have to be made in the first place? Is NASA protecting us from something? Are we not alone? We have all of these telescopes looking for signs of life out there in the Universe and it could be next door to us on the Moon. I'm sure that would rattle a few nerves, never mind leaders, hence keeping it a secret.

Apollo 16 was a mission that would reveal signs of something unusual. An interesting conversation took place and even footage exists of astronauts John Young and Charlie Duke discussing footprints. It really is one of those intriguing moments of the Apollo Missions that leaves you asking more questions:

Duke: "Look at that glass colored one right their John."

Young: "Pretty good size is'nt...."

Duke: "Yeh."

Young: "Look like it's about 3 days old, must be on the order of 4 billion."

Duke:	"Lets lift this one up and er, ah, rat…this looks like a company on errors on a tomb."
Young:	"Yeh."
Duke:	"Hold still."
Young:	"That is a crystal in a rock, if I've ever seen a crystal in a rock."
Duke:	"First one today."
Young:	"Yeh."
Duke:	"We've got to get over this John…."
Young:	"Do you want to take off and go that way know?"
Duke:	"Yeh. Hey John did you make those little footprints here on this sur….?
Young:	"Yes I guess I did yer I did."
Duke:	"Ah the old footprints on the crater rim."
Young:	"There's a good rock right there."
Duke:	"Look at the size of that rock. I thought this thing was right next door to us."
Young:	"Well there we have your half rock right there. It got black streaks coming out of it huh…"

The conversation continues and we are all left wondering why footprints were talked about in such a casual manner, considering we are supposedly the only one's on the Moon. There is an issue about those words, firstly "little footprints" and secondly "Ah the old footprints on the crater rim".

So excuse me when I pick out 'LITTLE FOOTPRINTS' and 'OLD FOOTPRINTS'. What does that conversation tell us? Is it possible that the astronauts were aware of something that may have been discussed previously? Were the footprints belonging to something of non human origin?

Lets look at another conversation that took place. It really does make you wonder just what was going on at the time.

Orion:	"Orion has landed. I can't see how far the [garble]..... this is a blocked field we're in from the south ray-tremendous difference in the albedo. I just get the feeling that these rocks may have come from somewhere else. Everywhere we saw the ground, which is about the whole sunlit side, you had the same delineation the Apollo 15 photography showed on Hadley, Delta and Radley Mountains...."
Capsule Communicator:	"O.K. Go ahead."
Orion:	"I'm looking out here at Stone Mountain and it's got- it looks like somebody has been out there plowing across the side of it. The beaches – the benches – look like one sort of terrace after another, right up the side. They sort of follow the contour of it right around."

Capsule Communicator:	"Any difference in the terraces?"
Orion:	"No, Tony. Not that I could tell from here. These terraces could be raised but of [garble] or something like that....."
Casper (Continuous Activity Scheduling Planning Execution & Re-planning):	"Another strange sight over here. It looks – a flashing light- I think it's Annbell. Another crater here looks as though it's flooded except that this same material seems to run up on the outside. You can see a definite patch of this stuff that's run down inside. And that material lays or has been structured on top of it, but it lays on top of things that are outside and higher. It's a very strange operation."

NASA of course says that all words used in this conversation are just metaphoric terms. The problem we have is that those words can clearly tell another story. Quite frankly to go all the way to the Moon and then use known vocabulary so clearly and say they are metaphoric terms does not seem believable. You have clear descriptions, "It looks like somebody has been out there ploughing" and "Hey John did you make those little footprints here on this sur..." Whatever you want to make of these sentences they speak for themselves and tell us something. We seem to have gone all the way to the Moon and misinterpreted the English language to cover up the truth. As we have discussed previously, NASA appear to have used secret codes, different channels and unclear dialogue.

Going to the Moon was without any doubt a great achievement and those men were very brave, but they were well educated and trained so all sentences were spoken with intelligence and truth. They saw things that were not natural, that were not that old and that also appeared to belong to non human origins. Conversations would indicate that these were known about already. You really have to give credit to those men who went to the Moon, not only was the job dangerous but they had to keep secrets as well. Somebody out there wanted secrets to stay that way and without a doubt, with military involvement it was not worth crossing their path.

So what if Apollo and all its missions found something? Whether they expected this or it was just a big surprise, it does not really matter because they did not tell the public. The Moon was already visited, and had clear indications of that. I'm almost certain there is still somebody on the Moon. The following conversation from the Apollo 15 Mission talks about tracks:

Scott:	"Arrowhead really runs east to west."
Mission Control:	"Roger, we copy."
Irwin:	"Tracks here as we go down slope."
Mission Control:	"Just follow the tracks, huh?"
Irwin:	"Right we're [garble]. We know that's a fairly good run. We're bearing 320, hitting range for 413..... I can't get over those lineation's, that layering on Mount Hadley."
Scott:	"I can't either. That's really spectacular."

Irwin:	"They sure look beautiful."
Scott:	"Talk about organization"
Irwin:	"That's the most organized structure I've ever seen!"
Scott:	"It's [garble] so uniform in width."
Irwin:	"Nothing we've seen before this has shown such thickness from the top of the tracks to the bottom."

An amazing conversation. Clearly both astronauts had found something. This whole business of tracks on the Moon continues with photographs of certain objects actually moving across the Moon's surface - Ref [PLATE 23 NASA PHOTO LO V,NO 67-H-1135]. I would like to make it clear that on an official level this picture is described as a meteorite skimming along the surface of the Moon. Other photographs indicate that this object changed direction. I do think it does look more like a tracked vehicle than a meteorite on this occasion.

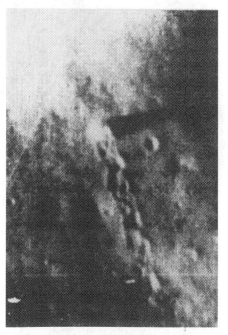

PLATE 23 [NASA photo LO V]

There are many pictures of surface activity on the Moon. Shown on the following picture, the movement can be explained as just rock movement or even a meteor skimming the surface. The Moon is millions of years old and has past activity and as we have been discussing, still has activity even in recent times. The picture has a logical explanation, whereas the previous picture was not as easy to decipher as a meteor.

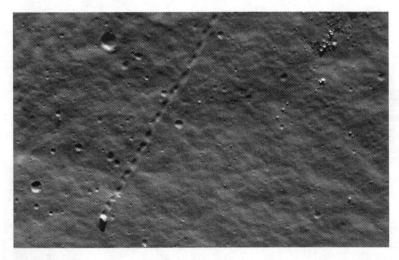

Rock or meteor?

What should be also brought back to our attention is what Major Patrick Powers said [Head of the United States Army Space Development programme] back in 1968, "The first man to reach the Moon must be prepared to fight for the privilege of landing". A statement like that in itself tells us that someone or something else is on the Moon. Doctor Carl Sagan was already convinced that the Moon had previously had occupants and that there were plenty of signs that they were still there.

How much evidence had been covered up? It seems the astronauts were clearly looking at evidence of life, as so many conversations were either being blocked or were in obvious code. Let's not forget that NASA is a civilian agency but part of the money for projects comes from the Department of Defence and that most astronauts are military officers subject to military regulations. This in turn connects us to the NSA [National Security Agency] which monitors all the transmissions and looks over all the footage from missions. Information is almost zero to the public and if you want to keep a secret then the NSA knows how.

Let's get back to the Apollo Missions and even more unusual conversations as the following dialogue reveals on the Apollo 17 Mission:

Mission Control: "Go ahead, Ron."

Evans: "OK, Roberts. I guess the big thing to want to report from the back side on this one is that I took another look at –the-cloverleaf in Aitken with the binocs. And that southern dome [garble] to the east."

Mission Control: "We copy that, Ron. Is there any difference in the color of the dome and the Mare Aitken there?"

Evans: "Yes, there is…That Condor, Condorsey, or Condorecet or whatever you want to call it there. Condorecet Hotel is the one that has got the diamond shaped fill down in the uh-floor."

Mission Control:	"Robert. Understand. Condorcet Hotel."
Evans:	"Condor. Condorcet Alpha. They've either caught a landslide on it or its got a- and it doesn't' look like [garble] in the other side of the wall in the northwest side."
Mission Control:	"OK, we copy that Northwest wall of Condorcet A."
Evans:	"The area is oval or elliptical in shape. Of course, the ellipse is toward the top"

That conversation was about domes, which back in the 1950's seemed to be popping up and disappearing in all sorts of places on the Moon. It seems that they are a mystery in most astronomers eyes, yet one subject I find very much one sided when conclusions are given. The Moon has some big secrets that are being shared with only a few, what does interest me is that whoever is on the Moon does not seem to be a threat. The Moon has had probes from both the USA and Russia and more recently from China and India. There are reports documented and filed out of sight that indicate that we were well monitored in space, but never threatened. The Moon is strategically positioned as an ideal observation post for looking at earth. Of course, the other side of the Moon could hide many secrets and that is the most likely place to find intelligent life as quoted by Carl Sagan in 1962 and Dr. Walter Riedel the late director of the Peenemunde Base in Germany.

With the abundance of materials on the Moon what's to say it's not already being mined? There's more than enough evidence to back that up. Back in the 90's, whilst looking at NASA archives, I came across pictures taken on two separate occasions from different lunar orbiters of the same crater. What surprised me on the later picture was that something had appeared which was not on the earlier photograph. It had the appearance of a crane involved in some form of mining work. When I tried to access the same pictures at a later date, they had disappeared from NASA archives.

Continuing on this subject, west of the crater Aristarchus, [LUNAR ORBITOR IV Photo no. HR 157]. The picture shows a circular crater next to an almost triangular crater. Do you not get the feeling that something is amiss? Whenever somebody makes a discovery in space, whether it is on the Moon or Mars etc. you feel as though they have been briefed to release the minimum of information and the rest remains a secret. One of the major changes in the space race since the Soviet Union disbanded is that the new Russia has been very open in areas of space exploration and has released documents and pictures of very unusual encounters in space. I'm not saying everybody in NASA is part of a huge conspiracy to fool us all, however I do believe that evidence should be more clearly explained.

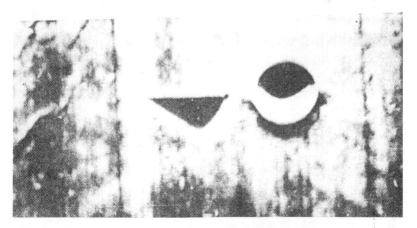

LUNAR ORBTOR IV photo HR 157

The whole set up is wrong, it seems everything has to be assumed as natural, even if the evidence points to life and clearly contradicts the usual protocol. The fact is that NASA and Russia do have official photographs of a lunar base which are kept in their secret archives. To add to this, secret filming and photographs by the Apollo astronauts captured evidence of structures, tracked vehicles and more unusual phenomena. We have already had an insight into how far covering up of information goes, but at the same time found the discrepancies. These become the jigsaw that we begin to join together, revealing the space program to be an expensive cover up. I spend a lot of time looking at pictures, reading reports and receiving information, many of which contain a lot of discrepancies. These make you examine the material more than you would normally, revealing new avenues and creating more questions.

Without a doubt, the Apollo Missions created debate and discussion albeit for the wrong reasons. We went to the Moon and returned, but at the same time the veil of secrecy that surrounded these space explorations only went on to fuel rumours that the Apollo Missions were all lies. There are too many errors for everything to be ignored. Errors create interest and that leads to conclusions of foul play. So here we are now looking further than before at what really happened on the Moon.

It really is easy to point the finger at NASA all the time, but the USSR was just as good at not saying anything. Back in the 90's an interesting picture surfaced [Photograph USSR orbiter 1960's] showing the Mare Imbrium area of the Moon. This can be easily seen from earth with a good telescope. The unusual features are rectangular and not your usual shapes, almost like a C shape. We decided to try looking at this ourselves using a telescope and the results were the same, showing a rectangular shape, looking out of place.

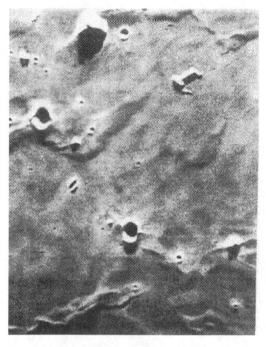

Strange shape top right [Photograph by USSR probe 1960s]

It's not so fair on those astronomers who have tried to make a point but have been shunned into the corner by other astronomers. Astronomer Gruithuisen's puzzle of a lunar fortress which created a huge debate at the time and Professor William H. Pickering's observation of a snow storm on Mount Pico [PLATE xxxiib], this would point to some kind of atmosphere. Pickering's observations on their own were very valuable, one of those observations being south of the Mare Imbrium where you can find the crater Eratosthenes. Pickering repeatedly observed greyish spots moving around inside the crater. The many theories put forward were not that strange either, ranging from clouds to even vegetation.

It would sound almost absurd to most people to say there was vegetation on the Moon, but it does seem that something very similar had been found. I must remind everybody reading this book that you only see one side of the Moon. It is suggested, without revealing names, that the other side of the Moon has more activity on it than you could ever imagine. There are again some very unusual photographs out there which do appear to show vegetation. NASA and the Russians have these pictures but are not willing to share them because they know exactly what the implications are.

CHAPTER 3

DRILLING THE MOON

At the end of 2006 it was announced in the media that we would return to the Moon. After all those years it seemed we were finally going back in the hope that we might live there and use it as a base to travel to Mars in years to come. This all becomes very interesting. If you have a Moon that already has occupants, we have either made a deal or this is one giant leap. The most difficult aspect of this for the NSA [National Security Agency] will be other countries who may be intending on visiting the Moon. You have India, China, Japan and the Europeans planning all sorts of pioneering trips to the Moon and they will include human beings.

Whatever the agreement made, if at all, it will be interesting how they pull it off. To be fair the Moon is a big place and we are only shown small areas, so if you want to hide something it should not be a problem. Perhaps everybody is after a part of the Moon, big money if you can use its endless resources. Back in the 80's it seems NASA had big plans for colonising the Moon. In 1986, Alamos National Laboratories presented the 'Subselene' a device for tunneling under the Moon's surface. The machine would be in the shape of a rocket, using a nuclear reactor. The idea was that heat produced from the reactor would melt glass-walled tunnels, which would be used for high-speed transportation. Because the Subselene could produce glass-like material, this could also be used for making bricks for construction on the Moon's surface. If you don't mind the technical jargon then this is how this device would work.

The nuclear power source would come from a very small SP-100 fission reactor. This would deliver heat to the tunneler head from liquid metal pipes, using lithium. Heat produced would not only

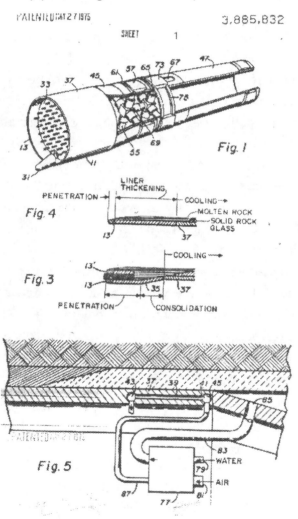

Patented May 27 1975 SUBSELENE SP-100

provide away of melting the soil and rock, but also power the mechanics and electrics. With cutting diameters of 3m and 5m, 260ft a day would be possible. Two devices were planned using the SP-100 fission reactor. After arriving and landing on the Moon, the device would bore to a depth of about 65ft. From this point it would level and create a tunnel. When all tunneling was complete, manned crews could take over and anything possible could be created in the tunnels, from mining to scientific study to even agriculture. Of course it would be difficult to say if this device ever left Earth, patented in 1975 and on the drawing board it possibly stayed. This may have been used or still in use on Earth. Due to its speed and efficiency it is an ideal machine for underground tunneling.

There is evidence that this system of drilling is in use, or something very similar on Earth. Reports of underground bases continue. The methods of drilling report of a device very similar to the Subselene SP-100 being used. The nuclear Subterrene was designed at the Los Alamos National Laboratory in New Mexico. This was followed by the United States Atomic Energy Commission back in 1972, taking forward the patent for the Subterrenes drill.

The nuclear Subterrenes melts its way through the soil and rock. As the device moves along it creates a glass lined tunnel. A nuclear reactor provides the heat which can both create the lining and fill cracks at the same time. Because of the pressure created by the machine it produces the cracks and hence fills them enabling the lining of the tunnel to continue. Liquid lithium circulates from the reactor core to the tunnel, where the rock is melted. It is then circulated back along the outside of the machine to help cool the vitrified rock as the machine moves forward. The cooled lithium then goes back to the reactor and we are back at the beginning again. This system of recycling and melting eliminates the process of removing the debris. The amount of waste associated with standard boring drills is huge, creating vast amounts of waste. Remove this factor and you can also go almost undetected under ground.

A system like this opens a whole new area of underground exploration. The big question is, is it in use? People have reported unusual vibration under the ground in different areas of the world. This has usually followed by suspicion of underground work being carried out. In some cases people working on these projects have leaked information, revealing that they exist and are used for part of a secret underground project. It is rumored there are hundreds of underground facilities on Earth.

We move forward to 1975 and the two new drilling machines are patented, one of these being the Subselene SP-100. It was a patent issued to the United States Energy Research and Development Admin.

Whatever the conclusion reached here, we still had patents showing drilling machines capable of boring through the ground effectively. Rumours have it that devices like these have created many secret underground facilities.

Some of those include The Dulce, New Mexico base and the following:

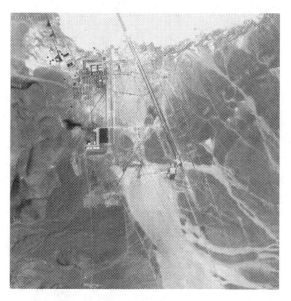

Area 51.

Denver Airport

I do believe we are using this technology and have most likely utilised it to the Moon. Crazy I hear you say? With the drilling machines being of a rocket shape, you can imagine it being transported with ease for use on the Moon.

CHAPTER 4

LIFE ON THE MOON

There is something incredible going on and as we have discussed in other chapters, anything is possible. That brings us to the big question:

Did we still keep going to the Moon?

I rather feel tempted by that phrase 'the show must go on". That show of course could have been the whole Apollo program in its well edited version screened to us. There is talk of Apollo 18, 19 and even a 20. Whether or not they are just rumours from the past, it is difficult to say. There certainly is an amazing Apollo 20 film doing the rounds, but again we are faced with whether it is fake or not. It does show Apollo 20 on a mission to investigate an ancient space ship and recover an Alien body. If fake, it is a good one.

What I have found really fascinating over the years are the amount of books published that mention vegetation on the Moon. Most people seem to laugh at any suggestion that the Moon is more than just a silent body and that anything is growing upon its surface. Going back in time to the 1900's a well respected astronomer W.H. Pickering had observed very strange dark areas that moved every monthly Moon cycle. The observations were seen especially in the crater Eratosthenes. Now what Pickering did next was quite something, he put his reputation on the line with the following statement:

"It is perfectly obvious that terrestrial vegetation could not exist on the Moon and probably not on Mars. But something does nevertheless exist on both of these bodies, which, while differing more or less from anything with which we are familiar, can be better described by the word vegetation than any other in the English language."

Pickering had without a doubt took a risk, but was certain that what he saw was what he had concluded.

This reminds me of the Apollo 8 photographs which were taken on the lunar back side [REF PLATE44,45]. What they seem to show is the Moon in autumn colours. This may sound mad, however what are we looking at? Vegetation? It's even more interesting to read that William Coopers [Ex US Navy] makes comments in his book 'Behold A Pale Horse'. He talks about areas on the Moon that change in colour and vegetation grows. He goes further and refers to manmade lakes and even clouds, something we have already discussed. Cooper even says he has the original photographs taken by NASA. It is very difficult to imagine a Moon that for so long has been portrayed as dead having some earth qualities. We seem to just take for granted what we are told, and if it does not directly affect us, then so what? I find it very difficult when astronomers and scientists say "not possible" and the next moment they are wrong. It seems there is a lot of evidence to say the Moon is not as dead as we are made to believe. For information, the lunar pictures Plate ref 44,45 are available online to view in colour.

At one time and in many astronomers' books it was said that water did not exist on the Moon and of course they were wrong. Information tends to be released a little at a time and by the time the public have got used to new information about the solar system, the silence resumes. However the information is still available for analysis. Very small news articles tend not to create much interest, yet the bigger stories are kept secret. Let's put a few questions in the air:

'What if we have a base already?'

'Have we already found intelligent life?'

'Are we jointly sharing the Moon?'

'Who is in charge?'

'Why all the secrets?'

'How far do you go with lies?'

'Where are all the benefits to mankind?'

'Is technology from somewhere else?'

In general sense all the above are accountable and apply. It's rather interesting when you look back at NASA and its general attitude towards the Apollo program. It was criticized for failing to provide scientists on Apollo Missions. It was not until after Apollo 14 arrived in lunar orbit when comments were made by Eugene Shoemaker (a leading figure in lunar science), who at a news conference told

NASA what a miserable job they were doing and that it was a waste of 24 billion dollars. NASA knew of Shoemaker and his general criticisms and others in the scientific community and had a plan to focus more on the geology in the next three missions.

As we know on the Apollo 17 Mission, the first geologist to walk on the Moon was Harrison Hagan Schmitt. He may have been on the last mission, but his geology skills paved the way for many interesting finds. What we must not forget is that there was going to be an Apollo 18 and 19, these missions would of explored areas of the Moon which would have been of great scientific interest. Due to lack of funding and public boredom the Apollo program was cancelled. You do feel though that perhaps NASA was leaned on by powers unknown as they were getting a bit too keen to explore further on the Moon than would have been allowed.

It is interesting to read in quite a few books that the Americans supposedly have a Moon base shared with Russia. There is no real evidence to confirm this, but when certain sources were questioned over this matter, the probability of this being true was 85%. What was even more of a surprise was that we were not alone, but sharing with non-humans. I must say that it does not surprise me to hear this, when you look at all the unusual conversations between astronauts and pictures which show strange objects you can easily get a suspicion of something questionable going on. This brings me to more of the unusual photographs which are available in the public domain, which I must say are odd. We enter the business of mining again and bridges and weird symbols and even letters. One of the most interesting pictures I have come across is a photograph of a crater [not named] that seems to show a white cross within it. What is even more interesting are the unusual terraces, which almost look as though they have been cut with some sort of machine. To go even further there seems to be a very strange black mark running central to the crater, just like a bridge. When you think back to Dr H.P. Wilkins at the Mount Wilson Observatory, USA and his observation of a 12 mile long bridge, it does not seem that crazy to suggest this particular crater could have one as well.

This picture could easily be passed for some mining operation on Earth. Look at the similar markings and almost road like tracks. Combine this with the fact that astronauts have reported tracks being seen, as well as lunar orbiters photographing moving vehicles - then you do have a lot of evidence to back up the possibilities.

I must point out that I am only talking about a small amount of pictures here and these are the hardest to justify as NASA and the NSA has gone to great lengths to make sure what is released will not give anything away. Remember the images they actually have would change everything and I'm sure a few shockwaves would follow.

Unknown crater photo Apollo 10

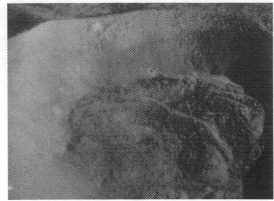

Area blow up of unknown crater Apollo 10. Observe the cross like object to the middle right. Strange dark line central, with unusual lines.

It's always fascinated me the amount of pictures you come across of the Moon's surface that show letters on them. We go all the way to the Moon and find not dust but plenty of letters. What fascinates me is the fact that most of these letters are from our own alphabet. You wonder if the areas are marked, so from an aerial view you can locate positions easily. Here on planet Earth it has always been a good way of locating things, people etc, by leaving signs on the ground to be seen from the air. Of course it all could be natural, but I would not be writing this book if it were that simple. It is very easy to say 'you are wrong' and that everything I have talked about is nothing but farfetched fantasy but that's the easy option! Those in charge will pull the wool over your eyes if they can get away with keeping a secret.

I remember years ago somebody saying to me that the Apollo Moon landings were all filmed on Earth and that it could be proved through the position of light on the astronauts and poor photographs. I do not really want to get involved in that area of the Apollo story, everybody is entitled to there own opinions and conclusions. What I would like to point out though, is that perhaps it was a cover story put out there to distract away from what was really happening. If NASA was willing to speak in code, communicate on different channels and keep photographs from us they must have had a massive reason.

Colonising the Moon is the intention of the Americans anyway, so whatever the outcome some secrets will have to be given away. It was not that long ago when people like American Author, Richard Hoagland were arguing the point of glass structures on the Moon and I must say with a lot of evidence. He showed photographs and pointed out the usual problem of missing pictures. NASA, it seemed, was very good at misplacing important photographs when you needed them and having strategically placed smudges. When you consider how many pictures were taken and how many we were actually shown, you do wonder what are on the others, which are either locked away or have been destroyed.

I personally think that Richard Hoagland brought an amazing insight of the possibility of glass structures on the Moon, which would be far stronger than certain metals in space. On Earth people experiment with the glass structure theme, staying months within them to find out if it is possible to survive in this environment. Therefore it is possible that this is all happening at this moment on the Moon. It does seem that 1972 was not the last time we walked on the Moon, nor 1969 the first time. Everything I talk about does not point to a silent Moon but a very busy one.

We are only showed what is acceptable, as the unacceptable is the truth.

Some of the following pictures show the unusual. The letter 'S' seems to be found on many pictures. It is either an illusion or maybe an indication of past visitors. The Apollo 15 photograph of the unusual crater to the centre, could be natural or even a nuclear explosion. It may sound farfetched but this has been discussed at higher levels. This brings us to this rather amazing Apollo 16 photo. The picture shows the lunar lander [John W. Young, Charlie M. Duke] moving away or towards the lunar obiter [T. Kenneth Mattingly II]. When the picture is focused on the cratered area to the left, we see an unusual object sat within the crater – cigar shaped and seemingly hovering over something. I would definitely say the cigar shaped object is for real, but underneath may be photographic pixels causing the unusual shapes. Nevertheless it is clear enough to see and under close scrutiny is classified as a UFO until proven otherwise.

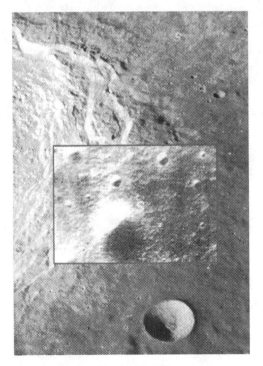

The letter 'S'

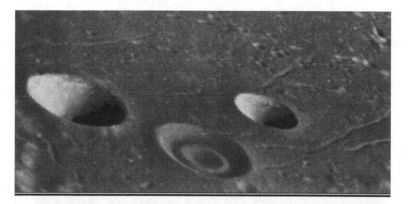

Apollo 15 N° 12640 - unusual crater to the centre.

Apollo 16, 1972. Area blow up of unusual cigar shaped object in crater.

45

I believe that we are not alone out there and would be blind to presume we were. The Moon is so close and yet so far from our minds. It has been described as a spaceship to an object created from our own Earth in the beginning. Whatever you would like to believe it is special and will always be with us. I look up into the sky sometimes and find it just sends you in to a trance, as you relish over its beauty and wonderment. It is hard to believe that it is alive. So many out there continue to turn their noses away and ridicule those who dare challenge an old and established system. As we have discussed, how many people does it have to take before the other half listen? Look at the many people in our past who have challenged our ways of thinking, who were either mocked or even executed for their own beliefs.

I have said from the start that all options should be left open and discussed. The human race is very good at telling tales and for some reason will go to great lengths to cover up the facts. That I am afraid is exactly what has been done in the case of our neighbour the Moon. Back in the early 90's I researched UFO'S it was one of my favourite subjects and one which was to lead me down all sorts of unusual avenues. I researched all kinds of sightings with associates and many others following the same trails and reaching the same conclusions. Those conclusions without a doubt told us we were not alone and that we were well monitored.

I remember a story about a leading figure in the UK government, who was having a bad time with some sightings. He was so upset about what he knew that on one particular occasion he broke down in front of his friends. What he said was very shocking and straight to the point:

"We are not alone"

What he actually meant by his statement, was that our air space was invaded all the time by 'unknowns' and there was nothing we could do about it. It is worth remembering that if you do report anything to the MOD they usually reply by stating that what you saw *"is of no defence significance."*

With words like that you are left speechless. This could easily lead down the road to Military Projects, but alas the technology was far superior and Military Projects are not usually carried out over housing estates. So what am I telling you all of this for? The answer is very simple. When we went to the Moon we were monitored on all occasions and some astronauts have admitted this. Photographs were taken and even film exists of close encounters of UFO's. There are many television programs that cover this subject now and hopefully will go further and investigate the real mysteries behind the Moon. We need to know the honest facts as information only becomes harder to decipher in the long term search for the truth.

Years ago Neil Armstrong narrated a series which was about the history of aircraft. It was very well presented and gave you a great insight into our achievements in flight. What I found really interesting was his description of the Lockheed F117 stealth bomber, which he referred to as *"Alien looking."*

I know it could easily be an innocent sentence, but you almost feel he had witnessed something alien to be able to give the comparison.

Stealth Lockheed F117

Neil Armstrong is one of those astronauts described as seeing things on the Moon that were of unknown origin. Once again I would like to make it clear, with exceptions of a few astronauts, most were connected with the military. Therefore they were under strict guidelines that took away their freedom of speech on the matter. So it is very difficult for them to reveal the truth under the watchful eye of their silencers. It all sounds rather controlled and I do not doubt the high level of secrecy they had signed up to.

If we have already made contact then we have already gone to the stars. Technology is accelerating so fast, you wonder if some of it has been obtained through cooperation with other beings. Back in the 90s, I was very lucky to be invited to join an aviation society. This group of enthusiasts would meet every month at a club, based at a well known UK aircraft development base. Every month would see guests, who would talk about their particular aircraft subject. On one occasion we had two elderly aircraft designers who gave us a very interesting talk on aircraft design and what was to come. They were not allowed to say too much, for obvious reasons, but did pass round a new material for the next generation of aircraft. It was black on the outside and had a honeycomb centre. This material was incredibly light yet at the same time strong. The technology was stealth, but something far more incredible was to come in the 2000's. We have certainly advanced in areas of flight at an incredible speed, leaving you wondering if we have had assistance along the way.

This subject gives you the opportunity to meet so many people who have a story to tell or just give you a small insight to the other world of secrets. The following was a conversation with someone connected with a space agency at the time. Although very brief, it revealed that an astronaut walking past a hanger was quite shocked to see a type of spaceship which was not of the typical rocket shape. Later, he made a complaint as to why we were not using the technology he had seen. Of course whatever he saw was most likely not for the public domain. Was he looking at a saucer shaped object or a triangular craft?

This brings us back to the Moon, which is so close yet has a hidden side. Everything connects together somewhere along the line and the closer to the source you get the more the truth. It is almost ridiculous to think that whilst the Apollo astronauts were going to the Moon, there was technology out there far more efficient and safe and we were using it jointly with alien beings. Most people will probably laugh at this and I don't blame you for doing so, but this is probably true and we have some serious issues to think about.

I would once again like to remind you of what prominent people said in the past about the Moon:

Major Patrick Powers:	"The first man to reach the Moon must be prepared to fight for the privilege of landing."
Dr Carl Sagan:	"Mankind must face the probability that beings from elsewhere in the Universe have, or have had, bases on the averted side of the Moon."
Dr Farouk El Baz:	"Not every discovery had been announced."
Dr Walter Riedel:	Believed that 'intelligent life was on the Moon.'
Otto Binder:	Claimed 'unusual conversations had taken place between astronauts on the Moon.'

To follow on from Otto Binder and the conversations, let's remind ourselves of some very unusual ones:

Apollo 16 astronaut Duke:	"Yeh. Hey John did you make those little footprints on this sur...?"
Apollo 15 astronaut Irwin:	"Tracks here as we go down slope".

It is difficult to believe that all these people were saying everything just for the sake of it. All concerned were in prominent positions at the time and no doubts knew exactly what they were talking about. It is a shame that in later years, some of the above individuals joined the club of keeping a secret. To be fair though, in more recent times there have been a number of astronauts revealing to a wider audience the fact that official sources only tell their version of the story.

CHAPTER 5

APOLLO CLOSE ENCOUNTERS

We now know that the first Apollo Moon landing was a very close shave. On the final moments of landing, Neil Armstrong had to manually land the Eagle as the on board computer system was not operating correctly. His quick thinking averted a major disaster. Many would argue that in itself was the genius of Neil Armstrong and cool nerves. Both Aldrin and Neil had finally landed and prepared for the most important walk in human history. They looked out onto a very alien world, but one that was about to be conquered. It is now apparent that all was not as it seemed. It has been discussed that comments by Carl Sagan and Major Patrick Powell might have been more to the truth than one would have first thought.

Maurice Chatelain was a former space scientist, NASA Chief of Communications and designer of the Apollo spacecraft. His first job after moving from France was as an electronics engineer in the aerospace industry and space program with Convair, specialising in telecommunications, telemetry, and radar. In 1959 he was in charge of an electromagnetic research group, developing new radar and telecommunications systems for Ryan. One of his great achievements was patents for automatic flights to the Moon. Chatelain was offered the job of designing and building the Apollo communications and data-processing systems.

In 1979, Chatelain confirmed that Armstrong had indeed reported seeing two UFOs on the rim of a crater. "The encounter was common knowledge in NASA" he revealed, "but nobody has talked about it until now." Soviet scientists were the first to confirm the incident.

"According to our information, the encounter was reported immediately after the landing of the module," said Dr. Vladimir Azhazha, a physicist and Professor of Mathematics at Moscow University.

Chatelain went on the say "Neil Armstrong relayed the message to Mission Control that two large, mysterious objects were watching them after having landed near the Moon module. But his message was never heard by the public because NASA censored it." According to Dr. Aleksandr Kazantsev, Buzz Aldrin took a colour movie film of the UFOs from inside the module, and continued filming them after he and Armstrong went outside. Dr. Azhazha claims that the UFOs left minutes after the astronauts came out of the module on to the lunar surface.

Chatelain had a lot to say about other missions as follows:

- "All Apollo and Gemini flights were followed, both at a distance and sometimes also quite closely, by space vehicles of extraterrestrial origin-flying saucers, or UFOs, if you want to call them by that name. Every time it occurred, the astronauts informed Mission Control, who then ordered absolute silence."

- "I think that Walter Schirra aboard Mercury 8 was the first of the astronauts to use the code name 'Santa Claus' to indicate the presence of flying saucers next to space capsules."

It was different when James Lovell who was on board the Apollo 8 command module, came out from behind the moon and said for everybody to hear:

'PLEASE BE INFORMED THAT THERE IS A SANTA CLAUS.'

This happened on Christmas Day 1968 and not a lot was said afterwards.

Returning back to the subject of the Apollo 11 Mission, it seemed even pictures were circulating of what Armstrong and Aldrin had seen. The following picture was taken from the module before they stepped out on to the lunar surface. Interestingly strange things were stated at the time and mentioned in some books, possibly connecting them with what was outside. The light from the sun seems to be reflecting off this object in the distance. It appears to be round, but may even be cigar shaped, as it could be on an angle. The distance indicates that it is probably the same size as the lunar lander. Examining the photo frames available this appears to have disappeared on later pictures. If we connect the two stories it does make it more feasible that Armstromg and Aldrin were actually looking at something outside the lunar lander which was causing them concern. I suppose we can easily write all of this off as hearsay. I am sure the people who would like to think this was all a hoax would look at this differently and maybe come up with their own conclusions. I don't believe it was a hoax landing, but a well observed one at that. Arguably the questions that arise are intriguing. Are Armstrong and Aldrin actually being observed by aliens or is it by other human beings? As previously discussed, we were more advanced in space travel than was being made public.

Armstrong and Aldrin in 1969. Are they waiting for something outside?

The following conversation was not made public, leaving you questioning what the space program was really about.

Moon:	"Those are giant things. No, no, no - this is not an optical illusion. No one is going to believe this!"
Houston:	"What ... what ... what? What the h--- is happening? What's wrong with you?"
Moon:	"They're here under the surface."
Houston:	"What's there? (muffled noise) Emission interrupted; interference control calling Apollo 11"
Moon:	"We saw some visitors. They were here for a while, observing the instruments."
Houston:	"Repeat your last information!"
Moon:	"I say that there were other spaceships. They're lined up in the other side of the crater!"
Houston:	"Repeat, repeat!"
Moon:	"Let us sound this orbita ... in 625 to 5 ... Automatic relay connected ... My hands are shaking so badly I can't do anything. Film it ? G--, if these d--ned cameras have picked up anything - what then?"
Houston:	"Have you picked up anything?"

Moon:	"I didn't have any film at hand. Three shots of the saucers or whatever they were that were ruining the film."
Houston:	"Control, control here. Are you on your way? What is the uproar with the UFOs over?"
Moon:	"They've landed here. There they are and they're watching us."
Houston:	"The mirrors, the mirrors - have you set them up?"
Moon:	"Yes, they're in the right place. But whoever made those spaceships surely can come tomorrow and remove them. Over and out."

There is other evidence of a sense of confusion and hesitation. Before climbing out of the lunar lander both astronauts seem to be preoccupied with lunar phenomena outside. It had been discussed that it was either the effect of bleeding the pressure from the capsule before switching to oxygen tanks or maybe whatever was outside. The following conversation from the Tranquility base is confusing, but at the same time is not generally discussed in public:

Tranquility:	"Got it (garbled) prime rows in."
Tranquility:	"Okay."
Tranquility:	(Garbled).
Tranquility:	"Let me do that for you."
Tranquility:	(Inaudible).

Tranquility:	"Mark 1."
Tranquility:	(Garbled) "valves."
Tranquility:	"Okay."
Tranquility:	"All of the" (garbled).
Tranquility:	(Garbled) "locked and lock-lock."
Tranquility:	"Did you put it –"
Tranquility:	"Oh, wait a minute."
Tranquility:	"Should be." (garbled).
Tranquility:	(Garbled).
Tranquility:	"Roger" (garbled).
Tranquility:	"I'll try it in the middle."
Tranquility:	"All right check my (garbled) valves vertical."
Tranquility:	"Both vertical."
Tranquility:	"That's two vertical."
Tranquility:	"Okay."
Tranquility:	(Garbled).

It appears that something was interfering with their senses. The lunar gravity was always going to be the first port of call. Somehow things got back to normal, but 2 hours of confusion had passed.

Aldrin does talk openly now about his own experience on the lunar module. The following conversation is now general knowledge:

Aldrin: "The first unusual thing that we saw I guess was one day out or something pretty close to the moon. It had a sizeable dimension to it, so we put the monocular on it."

Collins: "How'd we see this thing? Did we just look out the window and there it was?"

Aldrin: "Yes, and we weren't sure but what it might be the S-IVB. We called the ground and were told the S-IVB was 6,000 miles away. We had a problem with the high gain about this time, didn't we?"

Collins: "There was something. We felt a bump or maybe I just imagined it."

Armstrong: He was wondering whether the MESA had come off.

Collins: "I don't guess we felt anything."

Aldrin: "Of course, we were seeing all sorts of little objects going by at the various dumps and then we happened to see this one brighter object going by. We couldn't think of anything else it could be other than the S-IVB. We looked at it through the monocular and it seemed to have a bit of an L shape to it."

Armstrong: "Like an open suitcase."

Aldrin:	"We were in PTC at the time so each of us had a chance to take a look at this and it certainly seemed to be within our vicinity and of a very sizeable dimension."
Armstrong:	"We should say it was right at the limit of the resolution of the eye. It was very difficult to tell what shape it was. And there was no way to tell the size without knowing the range or the range without knowing the size."
Aldrin:	"So then I got down in the LEB and started looking for it in the optics. We were grossly misled because with the sextant off focus what we saw appeared to be a cylinder."
Armstrong:	"Or really two rings."
Aldrin:	"Yes."
Armstrong:	"Two rings. Two connected rings."
Aldrin:	"Yes."
Collins:	"No, it looked like a hollow cylinder to me. It didn't look like two connected rings. You could see this thing tumbling and, when it came around end-on, you could look right down in it's guts. It was a hollow cylinder. But then you could change the focus on the sextant and it would be replaced by this open book shape. It was really weird."
Aldrin:	"I guess there's not too much more to say about it other than it wasn't a cylinder."

Collins: "It was during the period when we thought it was a cylinder that we inquired about the S-IVB and we'd almost convinced ourselves that's what it had to be. But we don't have any more conclusions than that really. The fact that we didn't see it much past this one period --- we really don't have a conclusion as to what it might have been, how big it was, or how far away it was. It was something that wasn't part of the urine dump, we're pretty sure of that."

The Apollo 15 Mission revealed that whilst the astronauts were on the surface of the Moon, they observed white objects flying past. This is recorded in the following conversation:

Capsule Communicator: "You talked about something mysterious ..."

Orion: "O.K., Gordy, when we pitched around, I'd like to tell you about something we saw around the LM (LEM or Lunar Excursion Module). When we were coming about 30 or 40 feet out, there were a lot of objects - white things - flying by. It looked as if they were being propelled or ejected, but I'm not convinced of that."

Capsule Communicator: "We copy that Charlie."

We are left once again wondering what the astronauts are looking at. Possibly a UFO encounter? A cloud? Or something else? I mention cloud as photographs were taken of white objects passing by, as shown in previous chapter. Many lunar surface photos reveal astronauts being observed by strange objects in the background. This following lunar photo from the Apollo15 Mission reveals an unusual object moving over a mountain. There are three photos which show the UFO turning. This is the best one of the three. Blown up on the second picture, it reveals more detail.

Apollo 15 astronauts under observation?

Close up of UFO

Many of the Apollo photos have blotches or marks on them. This does make it difficult to determine what is real or not. These particular pictures do not fit that category. UFO it stays. This object seems to be more delta shaped, rather than your typical saucer and cigar shapes. I think they knew who it was. The delta shape is a design we have used for a long time. Many sightings of UFO's describe triangular light formations and shapes. They usually are described as silent, able to hover and travel at shattering speed. This could be alien or alternatively a more advanced craft that human beings are using. Most sightings of UFO's on the moon seem to be either cigar shaped or saucer, so this does open up other questions.

We move onto some even more unusual conversations from the Apollo 16 Astronauts:

| Duke: | "These devices are unbelievable. I'm not taking a gnomon up there." |
| Young: | "O.K., but man, that's going to be a steep bridge to climb." |

Duke:	"You got - YOWEE! Man - John, I tell you this is some sight here. Tony, the blocks in Buster are covered - the bottom is covered with blocks, five meters across. Besides the blocks seem to be in a preferred orientation, northeast to southwest. They go all the way up the wall on those two sides and on the other side you can only barely see the out-cropping at about 5 percent. Ninety percent of the bottom is covered with blocks that are 50 centimeters and larger."
Capsule Communicator:	"Good show. Sounds like a secondary ..."
Duke:	"Right out here ... the blue one that I described from the lunar module window is colored because it is glass coated, but underneath the glass it is crystalline ... the same texture as the Genesis Rock ... Dead on my mark."
Young:	"Mark. It's open."
Duke:	"I can't believe it!"
Young:	"And I put that beauty in dry!"
Capsule Communicator:	"Dover. Dover. We'll start EVA-2 immediately."

Duke:	"You'd better send a couple more guys up here. They'll have to try (garble)."
Capsule Communicator:	"Sounds familiar."
Duke:	"Boy, I tell you, these EMUs and PLSSs are really super-fantastic!"

It is apparent that the astronauts are talking in code - meaning to disguise what they are referring to. The big question is why the excited cries? Can this be due to the collecting of Moon rocks as they would have us believe? Or did they find something much more substantial which was not meant for public knowledge?

Unusual rock or block?

The Apollo 16 Mission brings us a conversation on domes and tunnels. I think this has to be one of the most amazing conversations that clearly indicates that they were looking at more than rock samples. It is my belief that we have a clear picture here of a structure which is not natural.

Duke:	"We felt it under our feet. It's a soft spot. Firmer. Where we stand, I tell you one thing. If this place had air, it'd sure be beautiful. It's beautiful with or without air. The scenery up on top of Stone Mountain, you'd have to be there to see this to believe it - those domes are incredible!"
Mission Control:	"O.K., could you take a look at that smoky area there and see what you can see on the face?"
Duke:	"Beyond the domes, the structure goes almost into the ravine that I described and one goes to the top. In the northeast wall of the ravine you can't see the delineation. To the northeast there are tunnels, to the north they are dipping east to about 30 degrees."

The following conversation is Apollo 17. Ronald Evans was the Command Module Pilot who was orbiting the back side of the moon. Once again, domes are mentioned and we are left pondering over unusual words:

| Mission Control: | "Go ahead, Ron." |

Evans:	"O.K., Robert, I guess the big thing I want to report from the back side is that I took another look at the - the - cloverleaf in Aitken with the binocs. And that southern dome (garble) to the east."
Mission Control:	"We copy that, Ron. Is there any difference in the color of the dome and the Mare Aitken there?"
Evans:	"Yes there is... That Condor, Condorsey, or Condorecet or whatever you want to call it there. Condorecet Hotel is the one that has got the diamond shaped fill down in the uh - floor."
Mission Control:	"Robert. Understand. Condorcet Hotel."
Evans:	"Condor. Condorset. Alpha. They've either caught a landslide on it or it's got a - and it doesn't look like (garble) in the other side of the wall in the northwest side."
Mission Control:	"O.K., we copy that Northwest wall of Condorcet A."
Evans:	"The area is oval or elliptical in shape. Of course, the ellipse is toward the top."

I would not be surprised to see NSA rather than NASA.

Following on, another Apollo 17 conversation reveals strange communications. You do wonder what they are actually looking at:

Lunar Module Pilot (DMP): "What are you learning?"

Capsule Communicator: "Hot spots on the Moon, Jack?"

Lunar Module Pilot (DMP): "Where are your big anomalies? Can you summarize them quickly?"

Capsule Communicator: "Jack, we'll get that for you on the next pass."

Command Module Pilot: "Hey, I can see a bright spot down there on the landing site where they might have blown off some of that halo stuff."

Capsule Communicator: "Roger. Interesting. Very - go to KILO. KILO."

Command Module Pilot: "Hey, it's gray now and the number one extends."

Capsule Communicator: "Roger. We got it. And we copy that it's all on the way down there. Go to KILO. KILO on that."

Command Module Pilot: "Mode is going to HM. Recorder is off. Lose a little communication there, huh? Okay, there's bravo. Bravo, select OMNI. Hey, you know you'll never believe it. I'm right over the edge of Orientale. I just looked down and saw the light flash again."

Capsule Communicator:	"Roger. Understand."
Command Module Pilot:	"Right at the end of the rille."
Capsule Communicator:	"Any chances of - ?"
Command Module Pilot:	"That's on the east of Orientale."
Capsule Communicator:	"You don't suppose it could be Vostok?" (A Russian probe).

As the conversation continues, we are made aware of 'watermarks'. This is again very unusual as you can see from the next dialogue:

Capsule Communicator:	"Roger, America, we're tracking you on the map here, watching it."
Lunar Module Pilot (LMP):	"O.K. Al Buruni has got variations on its floor. Variations in the lights and its albedo. It almost looks like a pattern as if the water were flowing up on a beach. Not in great areas, but in small areas around the southern side, and the part that looks like the water-washing pattern is a much lighter albedo, although I cannot see any real source of it. The texture, however, looks the same."

Capsule Communicator:	"America, Houston. We'd like you to hold off switching to OMNI Charlie until we can cue you on that."
Lunar Module Pilot (DMP):	"Wilco."
Lunar Module Pilot (LMP):	"Was there any indication on the seismometers on the impact about the time I saw a bright flash on the surface?"
Capsule Communicator:	"Stand by. We'll check on that, Jack."
Lunar Module Pilot (LMP):	"A UFO perhaps, don't worry about it. I thought somebody was looking at it. It could have been one of the other flashes of light."
Capsule Communicator:	"Roger. We copies the time and ..."
Lunar Module Pilot (LMP):	"I have the place marked."
Capsule Communicator:	"Pass it on to the back room."
Lunar Module Pilot (LMP):	"O.K. I've marked it on the map, too."

Capsule Communicator:	"Jack, just some words from the back room for you. There may have been an impact at the time you called, but the Moon is still ringing from the impact of the S-IVB impact. So it would mask any other impact. So they may be able to strip it out at another time, but right now they don't see anything at the time you called."
Lunar Module Pilot (LMP):	"Just my luck. Just looking at the southern edge of Grimaldi, Bob, and - that Graben is pre-Mare. Pre-Mare!"
Capsule Communicator:	"O.K., I copy on that, Jack. And as long as we're talking about Grimaldi we'd like to have you brief Ron exactly on the location of that flashing light you saw ... We'll probably ask him to take a picture of it. Maybe during one of his solo periods."

This communication was very interesting because the Capsule Communicator confirms that it was a flashing light. The Lunar Command Module Pilot uses the word 'UFO'. It seems clear that both the astronauts and NASA take this sighting seriously. What the public are not aware of is that detailed photographs were taken of these incidents and areas of a map were marked for reference. The Apollo 17 astronauts were in discussion about watermarks right at the moment that the UFO sighting occurred. We now return to the conversation:

Lunar Module Pilot (DMP):	"O.K. 96:03. Now we're getting some clear - looks like pretty clear high watermarks on this –"
Command Module Pilot:	"There's high watermarks all over the place there."
Lunar Module Pilot (LMP):	"On the north part of Tranquillitatis. That's Maraldi there, isn't it? Are you sure we're 13 miles up?"
Capsule Communicator:	"You're 14 to be exact, Ron."
Lunar Module Pilot (LMP):	"I tell you there's some mare, ride or scarps that are very, very sinuous - just passing one. They not only cross the low planar areas but go right up the side of a crater in one place and a hill in another. It looks very much like a constructional ridge - a mare-like ridge that is clearly as constructional as I would want to see it."

The conversations of unusual activity seem to be well documented, but not really public knowledge. This of course leaves you asking more questions than ever. To even suggest any of this leads to alien interaction or even a separate space program, sends ripples of shock through the well ironed establishment.

From the Apollo 10 Mission we are even told of music on the hidden side of the moon. On day five of the mission, Astronauts Thomas P. Stafford and Eugene A. Cernan descended to an altitude of less than 47,000 feet above the Moon in the lunar module. Two passes were made over the Apollo 11 landing site of the future. Astronaut John W. Young in the command module practiced the maneuver required to connect the lunar module to the command module.

On May 24th 1969, the service propulsion system was fired up, and the astronauts began the return journey to Earth. There were lots of photographs taken and film, but no mention of the following music in any conversation. As important as it was, it seemed not appropriate to say anything.

The following are the tape transcripts:

Day 5 – Page 195 – Tape 10-03601 AS10 LM:

04 06 12 43	**Commander:**	"Hey, when do we fire the helium tanks? ..."
04 06 12 47	**Lunar Module Pilot (LMP):**	"Not yet, babe."
04 06 12 53	**Commander:**	"You want some more brownies?"
04 06 12 54	**Lunar Module Pilot (LMP):**	"No."

04 06 12 56	Commander:	"... go hungry."
04 06 13 02	Lunar Module Pilot (LMP):	"That music even sounds outer-spaeey, doesn't it? You hear that? That whistling sound?"
04 06 13 06	Commander:	"Yes."
04 06 13 07	Lunar Module Pilot (LMP):	"Whooooooo. Say your – –"
04 06 13 12	Command Module Pilot:	"Did you hear that whistling sound, too?"
04 06 13 14	Lunar Module Pilot (LMP):	"Yes. Sounds like – you know, outer-space-type music."
04 06 13 18	Command Module Pilot:	"I wonder what it is."
04 06 13 29	Lunar Module Pilot (LMP):	"Mine's all burned off. isn't that weird – eerie, John?"
04 06 13 34	Command Module Pilot:	"Yes, I got it, too .... and see who was outside."

Day 5 – Page 195 – Tape 10-03601 AS10 LM:

04 06 17 58	Lunar Module Pilot (LMP):	"Boy, that sure is weird music."
04 06 18 01	Command Module Pilot:	"We're going to have to find out about that. Nobody will believe us."

| 04 06 18 07 | **Lunar Module Pilot (LMP):** | "Yes. It's a whistling, you know, like an outerspace-type thing." |
| 04 06 18 10 | **Command Module Pilot:** | "Yes .... VHF-A ..." |

Day 5 – Page 235 – Tape 10-03601 AS10 LM

04 07 32 53	**Lunar Module Pilot (LMP):**	"Houston, we've got you on OMNI's. You hear music, Tom? That crazy whistling?"
04 07 33 00	**Commander:**	"I can hear it."
04 07 33 01	**Lunar Module Pilot (LMP):**	"That's really weird."
04 07 33 02	**Commander:**	"It is."

Day 5 – Page 237 – Tape 10-03601 AS10 LM

04 07 37 18	**Lunar Module Pilot (LMP):**	"It's 52.3."
04 07 37 24	**Commander:**	"What'd ground give us?"
04 07 37 38	**Lunar Module Pilot (LMP):**	"Am I glad we didn't torque up the platform."

04 07 37 41	**Commander:**	"How in the hell did we miss that?"
04 07 37 49	**Lunar Module Pilot (LMP):**	"We had to have someone on our side that time."
04 07 37 51	**Commander:**	"Yes."
04 07 37 56	**Lunar Module Pilot (LMP):**	"Listen to eerie music'"
04 07 38 00	**Commander:**	"You – You ready?"
04 07 38 04	**Lunar Module Pilot (LMP):**	"Yes..."

Day 5 – Page 238 – Tape 10-03601 AS10_LM:

04 07 38 49	**Lunar Module Pilot (LMP):**	"Boy, it got quiet."
04 07 38 52	**Commander:**	"Huh?"
04 07 38 53	**Lunar Module Pilot (LMP):**	"Didn't it? We still got thrusters?"
04 07 38 54	**Commander:**	"Oh, yes. Ready? PROCEED."
04 07 38 57	**Lunar Module Pilot (LMP):**	"Man, I tell you, it just got quiet."
04 07 39 33	**Command Module Pilot:**	"Roger."

04 07 39 47	**Commander:**	"Those numbers again, Gene-o, are what?"
04 07 39 57	**Lunar Module Pilot (LMP):**	"I'll put mine on, Tom."
04 07 40 51	**Lunar Module Pilot (LMP):**	"I tell you, John, that music is really weird."
04 07 40 55	**Command Module Pilot:**	"… Think we're going to get it on the front side?"
04 07 40 58	**Lunar Module Pilot (LMP):**	"Know it. You composed something, huh?"
04 07 41 03	**Command Module Pilot:**	"I don't know, man."
04 07 41 05	**Lunar Module Pilot (LMP):**	"No one will believe us. Okay, Tom, we're set until 35 minutes – 35 seconds…"

Day 5 – Page 237 AS10 CM

04 12 09 07	**Lunar Module Pilot (LMP):**	"Yes but the Gemini she21 was a lot sturdier and stronger than …"
04 12 09 10	**Commander:**	"… to the walls – you can see the freaking walls."

04 12 09 15	Command Module Pilot:	"I never would have taken my helmet off in that thing."
04 12 09 16	Commander:	"I mean you ... What the hell was that gurgling noise?"
04 12 09 25	Lunar Module Pilot (LMP):	"I don't know. But I'll tell you, that eerie music is what's bothering me. You know that –"
04 12 09 28	Command Module Pilot:	"God damn, I heard it, too."
04 12 09 29	Lunar Module Pilot (LMP):	"You know that was funny. That's Just like something from outer space, really. Who's going to believe it?"
04 12 09 34	Command Module Pilot:	"Nobody. Shall we tell them about it?"
04 12 09 39	Lunar Module Pilot (LMP):	"I don't know. We ought to think about it some."
04 12 09 41	Command Module Pilot:	"Did you hear it, Tom?"
04 12 09 42	Lunar Module Pilot (LMP):	"Yes, he heard it."
04 12 09 43	Commander:	"Yes."

04 12 09 47	**Lunar Module Pilot (LMP):**	"Hell, I Just want to get out of this suit."

An interesting communication, but not considered worthy of a mention. Annoying as it is, you feel once again that this would have given away too much. These transcripts are well published on the internet now, but still not featured on mainstream TV. I am sure it must have been frustrating for the astronauts to encounter something like this and then being ordered not to repeat anything. Could this have been sound coming from a Moon base? Or perhaps an object orbiting nearby? When incidents like this happen you do get a feeling that the authorities know exactly what they are dealing with and their answer is to remain silent.

CHAPTER 6

THE DUBBING OF APOLLO FOOTAGE

There is so much film from the Apollo Missions, some good some very poor. The number of videos, DVD and other documentary formats is huge. On looking closer you soon realise you are faced with either a mountain of errors or poor editing. This reflects on the accuracy of everything you are looking at. Some documentaries are made with what was available at the time and are not accurate, but made for entertainment purposes.

One of the greatest documentaries "For All Mankind" was dubbed. You have moving footage with different sound. This was due to the poor quality of sound recordings from the Apollo footage. This meant salvaging what you could from what was available, but not necessarily matching the original footage to the original sound. As all the astronauts were wearing a space suit, you could never see their mouths and therefore the footage was easy to dub. A good example is on Youtube, this shows the Apollo 17 astronauts moving down a slope to a large rock. This is known as the 'house rock'. They are singing a song and generally having a great time. This is actually wrong. The sound is Apollo 17, but the moving footage Apollo 16. To make things even more confusing there are more versions of this particular scene with different dialogue. NASA does have a site for you to check out all conversations. This is helpful, but again confusing. There are other productions of video available; to add to the confusion they are sold as correct versions when they are not. Nothing matches in this huge minefield of film and sound. It is almost silly to think we went all the way to the moon and back and yet are not editing the whole mission accurately. Youtube basically has hundreds and thousands of people watching Apollo footage that is incorrect. If you want a headache then this is free.

One other thing that does come to mind - is all this confusion just bad editing? Or do we have another agenda behind this? I suppose it is easy in this case to say it is just editing errors, but there are other factors to remember:

- The amount of unofficial conversations.

- Sentences that reveal more than just rocks and dust.

- The amount of incorrect documentaries.

- The question of creating confusion in order to keep a big secret.

I could easily dismiss all of this and just put everything down to bad editing. But it is always going to bug me that you can have so many different versions of something that everyone generally thinks is correct. There are so many unusual words "Footprints"... "Tracks"... "Domes"... "Lights"... just these few, have you asking more questions. If you put confusion in anything you have control. I do spend a lot of time looking at different pieces of Apollo footage and have help from other associates. There is so much to look at, you cannot do it yourself. I am always amazed that we take for granted everything we watch and listen to is genuine. Everybody needs to look again and past the words of so called 'truth'. Television as we know it, will always sell you a story whether the facts are accurate or not. That's the way it is in the name of entertainment. It is time to look at everything again and start from scratch. You will be truly amazed at what you missed before.

House Rock, Apollo 16 available dubbed in many versions.

CHAPTER 7

THE FUTURE

I would like to point out that on many occasions I have requested from NASA certain pictures taken either on, or in orbit around the Moon. Some departments were helpful, but were unable to provide the information I required. I have studied many pictures and subsequently sent them to a number of prominent people for their opinion, all of whom replied with phrases such as "keep up the good work" and "very interesting". Many of these experts seemed more baffled than I was at the apparent discrepancies. There are many people out there following the same avenue that I had decided to take and I wish them all good luck and hope that together we can solve the mystery in the end.

1969 and Neil Armstrong said those famous words, "That's one small step for man, one giant leap for mankind". If only those words were true. You could say it was one giant leap backwards, especially in keeping secrets and if it that meant silencing astronauts for life, then so be it. They were all never to forget their experiences of visiting another world which was to have such an impact on their lives back on Earth.

The evidence points to a Moon that has already been explored, showing signs of civilizations which may even still exist. We may even be secretly co-operating with another intelligent life form. Interacting with a higher intelligence has brought us technologies to expand our knowledge. If you think this sounds crazy then look carefully at how we have evolved in such a short period of time in the areas of technology. From the Victorian revolution in machinery to two world wars, we advanced at a fast pace. Aircraft revealed a jump from basics to engineering never seen before. Computers in the form of the microchip started to takeover our minds, whilst everything in medicine and science was accelerating towards a new perfection. Did we really do all this ourselves? Or was there always an Alien influence? We have advanced so far in such a short time, you wonder if many agreements have been made. You also question rumours of us already being part of a galactic fleet, travelling further than ever before. Starships may be a reality and not for science fiction anymore. Can you imagine if we already walk on other worlds?

Governments keep secrets in the name of defence. The defence of what? As I have said before, we are most likely to be already working on the moon and have been doing so for a long time. It is possible that different governments are co-operating with one or more alien species to carry out mining operations on the Moon.

The Moon is a world of valuable materials and offers a fantastic watch post for observing Earth. There will come a day when the world is more united and there will be no more secrets. This will be the day when the human race will be free.

HOW TO CAPTURE A MOON ANOMALY

I have always thought that publishing books and disseminating information is a great way for me to share the knowledge I have gained through many years of research work.

However, with a little time and effort we can all be successful investigators by following a few simple steps.

Your first route to exploring the moon is purchasing the following:

Binoculars   A reasonable pair of binoculars is all you need to get started. Many people choose to start with this option rather than jumping straight into using the more complicated telescope. Even a moderate pair of binoculars will reveal 7 times as much information as an unaided eye can see.

Telescope   Usually reasonably priced, available as refractor or reflector. This means you look directly through one telescope, whilst the other reflects on a mirror. They all come in different sizes. A 6-8 inch reflector is great with appropriate lenses. See online guides for the best lens. Remember when purchasing a telescope, the stand must be good quality as poorly made stands cause shake on the lens.

Adapters	If you want more from your telescope then you can connect a camera or video device through an adaptor. They all vary in price, so the more you pay the better the quality. These can connect to laptops and combined with a motorised telescope, you are able to sit and watch images on the screen.
Camera	The best cameras are those which have changeable lenses, enabling you to see further. A good example is a 70-300ml zoom which gives you an enhanced view of the object you are looking at.
Notepad and pen	The easy way to log anything. Be sure to also log dates, times, atmospheric conditions and if possible co-ordinates.
Voice recorder	Quick, easy and fast for recording accurate information on the go. Again, be sure to log the same vital information as you would with a notepad and pen.

Now you are set up, it is time to go out and explore. The Moon is not the easiest object to film or photograph in the night sky, so take note of the following.

Moon Filters	Great for using with telescopes for filtering through the brightness and sometimes getting more detail.
Full Moon	Not the best time to look as the glare can leave you looking at just a bright spot. The best time is when the moon is under half its size. Less glare and more detail appears.

Cloud	If cloud rules then you might as well pack up for the night.
Objects	The night sky has all kinds of objects in it – therefore it is wise to research meteors, comets, planets, stars and especially manmade objects. You have aircraft, satellites, space stations and all in between you and the Moon. It is best to know the basics first before finding an anomaly. Be aware that birds fly at night and can easily be mistaken for something unusual.

You should now be prepared for an adventure. One thing that comes to mind is to clean your equipment regularly. You do not want to observe dirty marks by mistake. If you are observing with binoculars or a telescope and even filming and photographing, always check weather conditions. It is also worth checking with space agencies what they have orbiting the moon. This narrows down the field of objects and opens you to the unknowns. A flash on the moon or an object moving unusually can soon become a good reward if you have carried out your research properly.

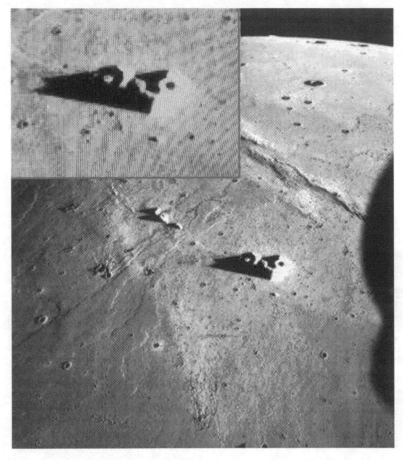

Moon anomaly or just the angle of the light? Investigating pictures can be a challenge. If you can do your homework properly, then you may discover a treasure to share.

APOLLO ASTRONAUTS

Apollo 7   1968   Walter Shirra, Donn F. Eisele, R. Walter Cunningham.[First Earth orbit]

Apollo 8   1968   Frank Boreman, James A. Lovell, Jr., William A. Anders. [First Moon orbit]

Apollo 9   1969   James A. McDivitt, David R. Scott, Russell L. Schweickart. [Earth orbit test of all modules]

Apollo 10   1969   Thomas P. Stafford, John W. Young, Eugene A. Cernan. [Practice landing for lunar landing]

Apollo 11   1969   Neil A. Armstrong, Micheal Collins, Edwin Aldrin, Jr. [First Moon landing]

Apollo 12   1969   Charles Conrad, Jr., Richard F. Gordon, Jr., Alan L. Bean [Second Moon landing]

Apollo13   1970   James A. Lovell, Jr., John L. Swigert, Jr., Fred W. Haise, Jr. [Failed Moon mission]

Apollo 14   1971   Alan B. Shepherd, Jr., Stuart A. Roosa, Edgar D. Mitchell. [First scientific visit to the Moon]

Apollo 15   1971   David R. Scott, Alfred M. Worden, James B. Irwin. [First extended mission]

Apollo 16   1972   John W. Young, T. Kenneth Mattingly II, Charles M. Duke. [First visit to Moon's central highlands]

Apollo 17	1972	Eugene A. Cernan, Ronald E. Evans, Harrison H. Schmitt. [Final visit to the Moon and the first professional scientist]
Apollo 18	?	Cancelled?
Apollo 19	?	Cancelled?
Apollo 20	?	May have happened and discovered Alien life?

A SELECTION OF GREAT ACHIEVEMENTS IN SPACE

- The Bell X-1. The Air Force supersonic research project. This craft was built by the Bell Aircraft Company. It reached a speed of 1000 mph in 1948.

- Yuri Alekseyevich Gagarin was the first man in the Vostok spacecraft to orbit the Earth on 12 April 1961. [USSR]

- Alan Bartlett "Al" Shepard, Jr. He was the First American to go into space in a mercury capsule in 1961. [NASA]

- Pioneer 10 was launched on March 3, 1972 and travelled through the solar system and beyond.

- Apollo/ Soyuz project. The USSR and US docked in space in 1975.

- The Viking program. Viking 1 launched August 20th 1975 and Viking 2 launched September 9th 1975. Both reached Mars and landed in 1976.

- Space Shuttle. Launched and first flight April 1981.

- The International Space Station [ISS] construction started in 1988.

5 STRANGE SPACE FACTS

- Neil Armstrong spelt backwards gives us an unusual surprise - GNORTSMRALIEN!

- There are dust clouds near the centre of the Galaxy that smell of rum and taste like strawberries. I'll leave you to work that one out.

- There is place in the Galaxy where there is 140 trillion times more water than on the Earth's oceans.

- There are 181,437 kilograms (about 400,000 lbs) of man-made materials lying around the Moon. Not a good advert.

- Mars is called the red planet. When the Hubble telescope photographed Mars for the first time, it appeared to have a blue atmosphere. Not so red.

THE GREAT SPEECH

It was a speech never to be forgotten. On September 12, 1962 before a crowd of 35,000 at Rice University football stadium in Houston, Texas:

"Its hazards are hostile to us all. Its conquest deserves the best of all mankind, and its opportunity for peaceful cooperation may never come again. But why, some say, the moon? Why choose this as our goal? And they may well ask why climb the highest mountain? Why, 35 years ago, fly the Atlantic? Why does Rice play Texas? We choose to go to the Moon. We choose to go to the Moon in this decade and do the other things, not because they are easy, but because they are hard, because that goal will serve to organize and measure the best of our energies and skills, because that challenge is one that we are willing to accept, one we are unwilling to postpone, and one which we intend to win, and the others, too."

John Fitzgerald Kennedy (Born May 29, 1917 – assassinated November 22, 1963)

"We live in a society controlled by a few, their decisions determine our futures. We live for them, but never see them, for they are not of this earth"

Simon Lewis 2015

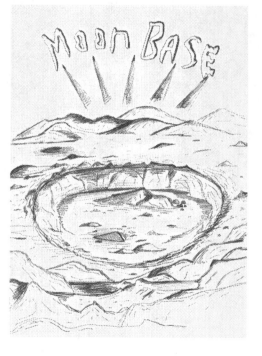

This is a short movie script, which some will find interesting and some will not. What we have here is a combination of events and information that may be true. This event may have happened or connects together some real facts and some science fiction stories. You are the judge; I am the writer, so you decide.

THE TWO FACED MOON

A spaceship orbits the moon. The spacecraft has the words LUNA 13 on its side. It is piloted by two Astronauts, James Lewis and Jack King, both very experienced in Luna exploration. The year is 1976. 24th June. 2100 hours.

LEWIS

Mission Control, Mission Control, do you copy?

MISSION CONTROL

Receiving you Lewis.

LEWIS

We are approaching the dark side. 2 minutes to radio silence. Advise over.

MISSION CONTROL

All systems are looking good. You are OK for decent.

LEWIS

Receiving you loud and clear.

The small spaceship now fires small thrusters which allow it to position for decent to the moon's surface. They plan to land in a crater known as Tsiokovshi, 150 miles in diameter, with steep walls and a massive central mountain area. This is considered to be a very dangerous mission.

LEWIS

10 seconds to radio silence.

MISSION CONTROL

Good luck Lewis, King. Hope the landing is a good one.

KING

Speak to you in 5 days. Changing over to auto-pilot.

The spaceship breaks contact and starts to descend. A central rocket fires as the craft makes its way towards the surface. The pilots continue to operate and check controls as it runs on auto-pilot.

LEWIS

When we're down there King, I'll be a lot happier. This is one hell of a ride.

KING

Yeah, I'll be glad when we're there too, this ship certainly is a bone shaker.

LEWIS

30 minutes to landing and counting.

KING

Main thrusters OK, pressure OK, computer readings OK.

The spaceship is now very close to the surface. The craters are now huge.

LEWIS

15 minutes to landing. What's your reading on pressure levels?

KING

Slight drop in pressure. Main thrusters OK. Positioning thrusters hanging in there. Computer reading are showing some unusual disturbances out there.

LEWIS

Probably nothing to worry about. Do you remember in practice, we had worse than this?

KING

Yeah, guess you're right.

The ship suddenly loses control. There's a small explosion on the outside. Oxygen starts to escape into space.

LEWIS

My God King, what was that?

KING

I don't know, but turn off the auto-pilot. We're losing pressure. Thrusters are not looking good. Electrical malfunctions.

LEWIS

OK, what about oxygen?

KING

Bad news, we need to get to the surface.

Both pilots press switches and look at a computer screen. The spaceship shakes violently.

LEWIS

We have 5 minutes to impact. Thrusters are almost gone. And that damn Tsiokovshi crater is coming at us like a raging bull.

KING

What about side thrusters?

LEWIS

No good, no good.

KING

Well there must be something. We're not going down without a fight.

LEWIS

Suggest something soon. Oh, God.

The craft suddenly stops shaking. There is a strange silence.

LEWIS

King?

KING

What's happened? I didn't do anything.

LEWIS

Neither did I, but look out of the window.

King looks towards a small window and sees a huge cigar shaped object. Still and silent.

KING

Am I seeing things or is that what I think it is?

LEWIS

Looks as though we're not the only ones who came here. And that's probably an understatement.

KING

Well understatement or not, something has just saved our lives and is not going anywhere.

LEWIS

Do you think it's ours?

KING

Well we've been briefed on this sort of thing. Never dreamed it would ever happen.

LEWIS

If it is ours, we're flying a dustbin in comparison to that beauty. I wonder if we should try to make contact. King and Lewis continue to peer out of the window. The ship is so big, their spaceship is tiny in comparison. The ship has many windows and huge round openings. In them can be seen smaller disc shaped ships. Lewis and King try to make contact.

LEWIS

I don't really know how to start. What should I say?

KING

Thank you sounds like a good idea.

LEWIS

Guess you're right.

Lewis fiddles with a few switches and speaks.

LEWIS

Hello, hello. Can anybody hear me? Do you understand English? We'd like to thank you for

saving our lives.

KING

No response Lewis. But there is movement. The radar shows something coming towards us. It's much smaller and disc-shaped.

LEWIS

Looks like contact has been made.

Both men look at each other. Around them lights flash and flicker.

LEWIS

Funny isn't it? Here we are, so far from Earth, no contact with them. We've just avoided hitting the moon and now we face, well something.

Suddenly there is a tapping noise. Both men look to the spaceship entrance.

KING

This is it then. It looks as though our saviours are knocking at the door.

LEWIS

Lets hope they are friendly.

The door makes a loud hissing noise. Both men look on as the door opens. As soon as the door opens they have gravity. Lewis steps forward. A small being, grey in appearance, 4ft tall with large black eyes, small nose, no hair walks towards them both.

LEWIS

Welcome. We are grateful for your assistance. Do you speak English? We mean no harm, we come in peace.

The small being is joined by another from behind. Their lips are small but seem to move. The first being holds out it's hand which has 3 fingers and what looks like a thumb. Lewis moves closer. They both join hands.

LEWIS

I think they're friendly.

The first being smiles. The second being points to the hatch. The men follow. The inside of the ship is small with no visible control. Just two small seats and a rounded ceiling of silver. Both men are shown an area to sit, rectangular seats appear from the wall of the ship. They sit down. The hatch closes. Movement of the ship is felt. It moves towards a large opening in the cigar shaped ship. Their spaceship is also moved somehow with a kind of energy field.

LEWIS

I wonder where they are taking us.

The ship suddenly jerks. A small click noise is heard. And the door to the craft opens. The two beings stand and one of them points to the door.

LEWIS

I think it's time to move. Do you notice, there's still gravity.

KING

Yeah I wonder how they got round that problem. Certainly beats floating around our ship.

Both men walk into a huge room where standing is a humanoid. Both are quite surprised.

LEWIS

I don't believe it, are you one of us?

JARKAN

Greetings. Welcome to our ship. Please do not be afraid, I can assure you, you are safe here.

KING

Do you have a name, and what about the two little chaps.

JARKAN

My name is Jarkan, and my small friends are my helpers. Or in your understanding, robots. They do not have names but numbers, which you will understand as Helper 8 and Helper 9.

The two small beings stand silently as Jarkan speaks.

LEWIS

I have to ask you just one question, are you from Earth?

JARKAN

No. I am from here.

KING

This is your world then?

JARKAN

Please, all your questions will be answered later. You are our guests and maybe you would like to freshen up before we speak again.

Jarkan turns and walks away. The two small beings point to a long passage. Lights run all the way down. The men follow the beings.

LEWIS

This ship is amazing. Look at the space. You'd get 25 of our ships in here with room to spare.

The men are shown to a small room. Suitable clothing water, food are there. The huge cigar shaped object is now moving towards a heavily cratered area of the moon. A triangular crater comes into view. Masses of light come from it as the ship descends. Around the unusual opening machines are at work. Inside there is a giant underground city. Lights shine from unusual structures and other objects fly within. The ship makes it's way to a large structure where it connects and comes to a halt. In the meantime, Lewis and King are freshened and clothed in unusual outfits and are led from the ship into the main building. They are then taken to a small room. Inside Jarkan greets them.

JARKAN

Please be seated. I'm sure you need an explanation. Please be patient and I'll answer all your questions.

The two small grey beings are stood to the side. Jarkan stands with a huge window behind him which has a view of the underground city.

JARKAN

Your ship was badly damaged but is being repaired.

KING

I guess we should be grateful that you turned up or we might not be alive now.

JARKAN

Yes gentlemen, but I'm afraid we were responsible for the damage to your ship.

LEWIS

What do you mean exactly?

JARKAN

You were going to land in an area where we are carrying out a lot of mining work and exploration.
It would not have been good for you to land without notice.

KING

I'm confused, you damaged our ship? And you're mining here? And all this technology?

JARKAN

We have been watching your progress as a race for a long time. You've advanced very quickly, especially in the last 100 years.

LEWIS

You mean you have been here that long?

JARKAN

Over two thousand years in fact.

KING

But why are you here?

JARKAN

I would like to ask you the same question? You have become very worrying as a race. War and power seem to be your main problem.

KING

But we are not all power hungry and killing each other.

JARKAN

Yes I understand that. But the people in power abuse and use the rest.

LEWIS

If you have been here so long, and watched us, why have you not helped us to evolve better?

JARKAN

We have tried on many occasions. Our ancestors landed on earth and communicated with many different cultures. We were received as what you call Gods. Which sadly followed by war in most cases, between themselves.

KING

What you're telling us, certainly fits in with many baffling stories and mysteries of our past, some never solved.

JARKAN

Yes, we probably had a lot to do with many situations that have occurred on your planet, but not just by us alone. There are about 25 millions different beings spread among the stars and many have been to your world long before we arrived.

LEWIS

What about God and religions. Do you have any answers?

JARKAN

Your God as you call it is the ultimate energy force and does create worlds and life. But as far as we know it is so far in advance than ourselves, we don't understand how it all works. You see the universe is far more complicated than we and you can ever imagine. Life as we understand it is a body and a soul. But passed that point there is an energy that is a life. But far more advanced than even we can imagine. Please gentlemen, we can talk about these things another time. Perhaps we should show you our world. Please look towards the window.

The glass window suddenly turns to a picture and different scenes start to appear.

JARKAN

This is our city. The structures are mainly made of glass and elements only known to us. The larger ship you can see moving out is our starship. Capable of travelling unimaginable distances. Powered by what we call clean energy. The small glass buildings are where we keep our plants, trees and food. All plant based. We have built glass structures before on the surface but due to the unpredictable meteor showers it created too many problems. The disc shaped craft is well known to you as a flying saucer and is used for short distances of travel. As you've already seen, it holds two helpers. We ourselves use the much larger ships. The helpers do most of our work.

Pictures are shown of humanoids and helpers, farming, mining and relaxing.

JARKAN

So gentlemen, this is our world. And has been for a long time. But we did live as you did a long time ago.

The screen disappears, the window is now restored.

LEWIS

Can you imagine if they all saw this on earth?

JARKAN

They already know. But only in your higher places. We have found them to be very difficult to deal with.

LEWIS

What do you mean?

JARKAN

We have had allsorts of accidents. The first major one you know as Roswell. 1947 was your year.

KING

But that was supposed to be a weather balloon.

JARKAN

Two of our helpers ran into trouble and had to crash land. Your military soon captured them.

Our cover was broken. Negotiations took place. Technology changed hands. You advanced very quickly with our help. How do you think you got here today?

LEWIS
You mean you helped design our ship?

JARKAN
In a way, most of the design goes back thousands of years to our early spacecraft.

KING
Did they know on earth about us coming here.

JARKAN
You ask so many questions.

KING
But did they know?

Jarkan turns and looks at the two helpers. One steps forward and speaks. Both men are surprised.

HELPER 8
The answer is yes. You two were chosen for your expertise and knowledge in Luna exploration.
Unfortunately, your landing coordinates where planned by people unaware of your governments treaty with us.

KING

What treaty?

HELPER 8

You were unaware of the purpose for your mission for security reasons. The real reason for your mission is for us to impart our knowledge to your peoples. You are trained in space flight. You are from Earth. You are the next step forward to bringing peace to your world. With our help, your world could become a better place.

LEWIS

All the while you are saying this, but you have already made it clear that we are power mad and always at war.

HELPER 8

You don't have a choice. Your world is dying. Your energies are nearly depleted. Your power base is collapsing. War could be your end. But not before world famine globally effects you all.

LEWIS

Why save us all if we have made such a mess? We surely cannot be trusted.

HELPER 8

If your world goes, our world goes. They are but one and one effects the other.

KING

You mean finally we have nearly done the unthinkable and reached our end?

Jarkan steps forward and Helper 8 moves back.

JARKAN

Yes your planet is badly damaged. Not just with the environment but war which seems to be everywhere. We have tried to help recently but communications can be difficult at times with your governments. When your ship is repaired you will leave here. But when reaching the other side of the moon your mission control will contact you. You will transmit a message and with that will be a film telling your people all about us. It will reach all screens across your world. Your people will see that you have to change for the good of all our races.

Lewis and King look at each other for a long moment and the scene ends.

THE FINAL SCENE

The men are seen next in their ship, moving away from the triangular base back into the moons orbit. The ship reaches radio contact.

LEWIS

Mission control, do you read?

MISSION CONTROL

Yes we hear you loud and clear.

LEWIS

Glad to hear your voices at last. We've had an amazing time but I guess you knew that was coming.

MISSION CONTROL

Did you get the information?

LEWIS

Yes sir. Ready to transmit.

Lewis looks at King. They smile. King presses a button. There is a huge explosion. The spaceship explodes into thousands of pieces. We return to mission control. Or what they thought was Mission Control. The signal had been intercepted on a secret channel.

Back at the moon city, Helper 8 and Helper 9 are sat in a room. Helper 8 touches a panel in front of him.

HELPER 8

Mission control to Lewis do your read?

HELPER 9

Mission accomplished.

ACKNOWLEDGEMENTS

Although I carried out my own study on the Moon, the following books were used for reference:

BEHOLD A PALE HORSE- William Cooper

GUIDE TO THE MOON- Patrick Moore

A MAN ON THE MOON- Andrew Chalkin

THE WORLD OF THE MOON- Henry King

OUR MYSTERIOUS SPACESHIP MOON- Don Wilson

MYSTERIOUS VISITORS- Brinsley Le Poer Trench

THE CONQUEST OF SPACE- Bonestell-Ley

THE MOON BOOK- Bevan M. French

A FIRE ON THE MOON- Mailer

THE NATURE OF THE UNIVERSE- Fred Hoyle

THE INVASION OF THE MOON 1969- Peter Ryan

FIRST ON THE MOON- Micheal Joseph

SOMEBODY ELSE IS ON THE MOON- George H. Leonard

THE TWO FACED MOON- Simon Lewis

A percentage of the pictures used are from the archives of NASA. All areas that show blow ups of pictures are my own work. All reports were purchased and original newspaper articles studied. Some pictures were purchased.

Printed in the United States
By Bookmasters